MOTHERS OF THE SOUTH

Portraiture of the White Tenant Farm Woman

MARGARET JARMAN HAGOOD

Introduction by Anne Firor Scott

The Norton Library
W·W·NORTON & COMPANY·INC·
NEW YORK

Books That Live
The Norton imprint on a book means that in the publisher's estimation it is a book not for a single season but for the years.
W. W. Norton & Company, Inc.

Library of Congress Cataloging in Publication Data

Hagood, Margaret Jarman, 1907—
Mothers of the South.

(The Norton Library)
Reprint of the 1939 ed. published by the University of North Carolina Press, Chapel Hill.
Includes index.
1. Women—Southern States. 2. Southern States—Rural conditions. 3. Share-cropping. I. Title.
HQ1420. H3 1977 301.41'2'0975 77-1696
ISBN 0-393-00816-9

1 2 3 4 5 6 7 8 9 0

Introduction to the Norton Library Edition

Mothers of the South is a book of the 1930s, and as such provides a dramatic reminder of the revolutionary changes in agricultural practice, life experience, social organization, values, attitudes, and expectations which have overtaken southerners since 1937. But it is much more than that.

Documentary expression, as William Stott has persuasively argued, was characteristic of the thirties. In an effort to get at the reality behind the statistics of the Depression, photographers, film makers, poets, and novelists joined sociologists and anthropologists to describe in their various ways the world as they perceived it. "The excellence of thirties social science," Stott writes, "was that it often captured the particularity and richness of ordinary life."[1] This *Mothers of the South* certainly does, and it belongs with *Middletown*, *After Freedom*, *Tenants of the Almighty*, as well as *These Are Our Lives* and *Let Us Now Praise Famous Men* and the photographs of Dorothea Lange and Walker Evans—all significant records of an era that is rapidly being lost to living memory.

The decision to bring out an inexpensive new edition of this work reflects the realization that this is not only one of the best nonfiction documentaries of its time, but also that it is a first-rate source for the social historian interested in now

1. William Stott, *Documentary Expression and Thirties America* (New York: Oxford University Press, 1973), p. 163.

almost vanished patterns of rural family life and work. The surprise is to find that the author of this book was best known as a practitioner of that most abstract of the social sciences—statistics.

Margaret Jarman was born in Newton County, Georgia, in 1907 and raised by a father who combined farming with scholarship and who had a special interest in the education of women. The fact that two of his daughters earned Ph.D. degrees is some indication of that interest. At sixteen Margaret Jarman was teaching in a rural school in South Georgia and giving violin lessons on the side. By the time she was twenty-three she had acquired two degrees, a husband (Middleton Howard Hagood), and a child.

Early in the 1930s she found her way to the University of North Carolina at Chapel Hill where Howard Odum, also a native of Newton County, Georgia, along with Rupert Vance, Guy and Guion Johnson, Harriet Herring, Paul Wager, and Katherine Jocher were making the Institute for Research in Social Science *the* center for southern regional studies and a magnet for young sociologists who wanted to combine scholarship with social action. Here Margaret Jarman Hagood embarked upon the work for her Ph.D., which she earned in 1937 with a detailed statistical analysis of the fertility patterns of native white women of childbearing age in the Southeast.

The study was an important contribution to the regional profile being developed by Odum and his colleagues. President Roosevelt, not long since, had called the South the nation's number-one economic problem. This group of scholars in Chapel Hill wanted to understand the social implications of southern poverty.

Demographers had pointed out that the Southeast, the least urbanized section of the nation, had the highest birth rate of any region. The more than twenty-two million native white women of childbearing age were destined not only to be mothers of the next generation of southerners, but, to a significant degree, of the next generation of Americans. In her thesis Hagood had presented the statistical picture; now she wanted to move on to the social context of the statistics. If so many children were being born on southern tenant farms, their life experience would be an important influence shaping the future of American society. "Farm tenancy" in this view was not only a problem for the agricultural economist, but for those concerned with the human resources of the country as well.

For sixteen months she traveled from tenant house to tenant house until, in all, she had visited 254 homes in the Carolina piedmont and in Georgia and Alabama, some of them several times. She listened, observed, and asked questions, to some extent letting the mothers themselves decide the direction of the conversation. Her subjects found her "not too far from former country ways to be able to understand." Since she had a child, they felt free to discuss childbirth. She was a woman, and so entered easily into the "distinctly feminine culture...centered on mating, child care and home-making," which she had postulated in her dissertation.

Hagood was too good a social scientist to draw more from her data than was justified and too sensitive a human being to turn her subjects into abstractions. She did not force her material into some a priori pattern of what was typical, nor mistake the unusual for the norm. Her prose was plain and forceful, and she wrote with the mixture of detachment and involvement which is the hallmark of good social reporting.

From her study we gain some sense of the variety of individual personalities subsumed under the general term "tenant wives," ranging from the twinkling thirty-year-old widow running her rented farm with the help of sympathetic male neighbors, to the distracted and despairing mother facing her thirteenth pregnancy. As we read, we realize that imagination and the ability to talk are not much related to schooling. We feel how strongly many of these people suspect city folk and city ways, and—the other side of that coin—the depth of their real love for the farming that rewards them so poorly.

Seven eighths of these women prefer field work to housework, and are prouder of their prowess in the field and in the tobacco shed than in the kitchen. We observe the variety of husband-wife relationships, and a curious kind of patriarchy which is honored as much in the breach as in the observance. The man should always carry the pocketbook, the women tell her, and the bossiest wife seems to believe herself subservient. There is no complaint about a division of labor that pulls women into the barn and field but does not allow men to help in the house.

We catch the echoes of frontier experience, with one enormous difference: these people do not expect the future to be better. We see remnants of the old cooperative patterns of corn shucking and barn-raising, and the ancient custom of plowing or harvesting for a sick neighbor, and wonder why these habits are on the decline in a time of deep trouble such as the thirties. We slowly grasp the fact that *no one* is in good health, and yet that none has taken to his or her bed (and none, she says, appears to be neurotic).

We see a family-centered life that begins early (the median age of marriage in her sample was eighteen) and forms the principal arena of experience. We observe a deep concern with raising children, though often the parents are in despair over their inability to provide for all their young, and note that even in desperate poverty there is no hint of child abuse. Indeed, there is a kind of understanding and warmth we might have thought was possible only for people under less exigent economic pressure.

We also see—as one northern reviewer after another noted with amazement—that southerners down and out in the South in the thirties, with little hope of ever being anything else, were strong, capable, and intelligent human beings. The stereotypes held by many northern readers had been formed by Erskine Caldwell's books and Margaret Bourke-White's photographs. Hagood took some pleasure in documenting another view of poor southern rural families.

Her book came out in 1939 and inspired mostly favorable reviews, North and South, popular and scholarly, many of which concluded with a stirring call to action: something must be done, the reviewers agreed, to "solve" the problem of farm tenancy. Marxist reviewers were delighted with what they took to be evidence that the South was ripe for revolution. Few—perhaps none—guessed that in thirty years the problems of southern agriculture would be transformed. Tenant farmers had numbered three quarters of a million in North Carolina in 1935; by 1970 they were so hard to find that the census takers had to develop new categories. In 1935 there had been almost as many tenant farmers of various kinds in the seventeen states the Census Bureau called southern as there are farmers in the whole United States today. Then came the agricultural reforms of the New Deal, mechanization, new crops, the stimulus of the Second World War. Poor tenant farmers, their wives, and children found jobs in war-related industry. Many moved to northern and western cities. After the war, machinery continued to replace people all across the South, so that the exodus to towns and cities continued. Between 1960 and 1964 an average of 376,000 people left southern farms each year. Poverty as bad as anything in this book still exists in the rural Southeast, but the structure of agriculture has changed beyond recognition and the numbers of people who are still sharecroppers and tenants in the patterns described in this book are few.[2]

Soon after *Mothers of the South* went to press, Margaret Hagood and her talented colleague Harriet Herring embarked upon a new project. With Dorothea Lange and Marion Post, photographers on the staff of the Farm Security Administration, they set out to make a comprehensive photographic study of thirteen piedmont North Carolina counties. Together these women photographed sharecroppers, houses and fields, churches, county courthouses, tobacco barns, tobacco auctions, eroded land, growing crops, and landlords, developing a visual image of the society and the economy of the region. Lange and Post took most of the pictures, while Hagood and Herring wrote up the accompanying text. An exhibition held at the University of North Carolina in May, 1940, showed the best of the pictures. "I consider it an opportunity for us to demonstrate to ourselves and others some of the potentialities of Photography as a tool for social research," Hagood wrote Roy Stryker of the Farm Security Administration.[3]

Meantime she finished her mammoth *Statistics for*

2. C. E. Bishop, "Rural Poverty in the Southeast," in *Rural Poverty and Regional Progress in an Urban Society,* Fourth Report of the Task Force on Economic Growth and Opportunity of the Chamber of Commerce of the United States (Washington, D.C., 1969), pp. 75-92. See also Robert Coles, *Migrants, Sharecroppers, Mountaineers* (Boston: Little Brown, 1971), for a sensitive study of present-day southern poverty, including that of sharecroppers, most of whom are black.

3. Margaret Jarman Hagood to Roy Stryker, March 27, 1940. Howard Odum Papers, Southern Historical Collection, University of North Carolina.

Sociologists, first published in 1941 and destined to become the standard introductory text in its field. She was also publishing articles in journals and becoming highly competent in population studies.

In 1942, Hagood left the University of North Carolina for the Department of Agriculture in Washington, D.C., to take charge of the farm population and related demographic activities in the Bureau of Agricultural Economics. In this capacity, and later as head of the Farm Population and Rural Life Branch, she made great contributions not only to the work of the USDA but also to the Bureau of the Census, the Department of Labor, the Department of Defense, and many other federal agencies. She was much in demand as a consultant on a variety of interagency committees that dealt with population and manpower matters. She authored and co-authored many government reports, journal articles, and papers, and instigated work in population projections, migration (using sources not previously exploited), studies of the farm work force, and the like that continues to this day. She was president of the Population Association of America and the Rural Sociological Society, was very active in professional organizations, and served in official capacities in the activities of many others. In addition, she consulted with the UN, traveled to the West Indies as a demographic consultant, and, with Daniel Price, revised her statistics text.

In the early sixties, she suffered a severe heart attack, after which she left government service, and in 1963, at the age of fifty-six, she died.

Margaret Hagood's friends and colleagues, asked to remember what she was like, nearly always begin by talking about how hard she worked. "Physical vigor, intellectual capacity, and drive," said one. "She didn't pay much attention to herself," added another. "Her intensity of purpose stands out as the motivating force in her remarkable career," said a third. Such single-minded dedication helps explain the amount of important work she managed to complete before her early death.

Part of her legacy must be the hundreds of social scientists who were, as one of them put it, "raised on her sociological statistics." Another must be her work for the benefit of farm families during the time she was in the Department of Agriculture. But surely an important part of that legacy is this classic study, which records those almost invisible women who, without much hope for themselves, persevered through the hardest times (in a society where hard times were the norm) and kept alive some values which are now, perhaps, about to be rediscovered. Theirs was an important segment of American social experience and one which, without Margaret Hagood's work, might have been lost beyond recovery.

ANNE FIROR SCOTT

Duke University
Durham, North Carolina

CONTENTS

Preface

THIS VOLUME reports a part of the work of one unit in the program being inaugurated in what is generally characterized the Subregional Laboratory for Social Research and Planning under the auspices of the Institute for Research in Social Science at the University of North Carolina. The present book is limited to a presentation of case material and a short summary of certain quantitative results. The more detailed statistical data of the study are a part of the body of records being accumulated on various aspects of the Subregional Laboratory in the Institute files.

Special appreciation is expressed to the two agencies making possible the study: to the Rosenwald Fund for the first year and to the Institute for Research in Social Science for assistance during this year and for its sponsorship and direction during the second year. Special acknowledgment is due to Dr. Howard W. Odum, Director, and Dr. Katharine Jocher, Assistant Director of the Institute, for their help at every stage of the study. Thanks are also offered to the secretarial staff of the Institute for preparing the typescript, and to Dr. Karl G. Pfeiffer for reading it.

It must be clear that it is scarcely possible to express full appreciation to all those mothers who so cordially gave of their time and their feelings to make possible the present work.

MARGARET JARMAN HAGOOD.

September 1, 1939.

Part I · Farms

Chapter 1

Of Farm Tenant Mothers as Symbol and Reality of the South

FARM TENANCY, for a long time a key problem, has recently assumed in America the proportions of a Number One economic dilemma. Nearly three million farms and over ten million people are encompassed in its sweep. In an unhindered trend toward farm tenancy will be endangered the basic principles of Jeffersonian America, namely, land as the foundation of national wealth and the sturdy landowning citizen as the bulwark of national strength.

Especially urgent is the case of those tenants who live in the Southeast, for here abide exactly one-half of all those in the Nation, and of nearly another half million in the Southwest. Yet not only because of their increasing number in the South, but also because of the increasing dilemma of their economic and cultural status, and because of their increasing share in the reproduction of the people, the assumption that Southern farm tenancy is a critical and dramatic problem of the Nation seems entirely justified.

For it is admitted that the South must play a major rôle in reproducing the Nation and that its obligation to translate its cultural and economic potentialities into a national contribution is great. One enthusiast in a recent conference carried his arguments to this extreme—"As goes the South," he predicted, "so goes the Nation. More than that, as goes the rural South, so goes the Nation. More than that," he exclaimed, "as goes the rural mother in the South, so goes the Nation!" This argument is after all not so unrealistic as it might appear; in fact, since over half of the Southern farms are tenant farms, it should be extended and adapted somewhat as follows—"As goes the Southern tenant farm mother, so goes a large part of the South and of the Nation." The query of this volume, therefore, "How goes the Southern tenant farm mother?" has pertinence and relevancy exceeding its immediately apparent importance.

Furthermore, such an inquiry may serve as a microcosmic examination of the wider regional scene; for Southern tenant farm mothers compose a group who epitomize, as much as any, the results of the wastes and lags of the Region. They suffer the direct consequences of a long-continued cash crop economy; they undergo extreme social impoverishment from the lack and unequal distribution of institutional services; and they bear the brunt of a regional tradition—compounded of elements from religion, patriarchy, and aristocracy—which subjects them to class and sex discrimination. Moreover, they continue to augment the pathologies of the Region by their very functioning, as they produce, at a ruinous cost to both the land and themselves, the cotton and tobacco by which the rural South still lives, and the children who are simultaneously the Region's greatest asset and most crucial problem.

If the South seeks to look at itself analytically and critically, intensive study of groupings is one way to provide data for the student of the Region. As a group for a unit of study in the broad research program on all the resources and wastes of the South, the tenant farm mothers embody many of the causes, processes, and effects of the general regional problems of an exploiting agriculture, overpopulation, general cultural retardation, chronological and technological lag. The interrelationships between the several areas of waste are so intricate and complex that no one aspect of the total situation can be treated separately. Yet our focus of attention is on these mothers as a unit of the present human resources of the South and as an important source of the future human resources of both the South and other regions of the United States.

The reasons for making this study and for writing this book, then, are evident. With regard to the collection and analysis of material, it is sufficient to say here that portraiture, cases, and examples presented reflect the part of Southern culture found in the Piedmont South. The group examined are white tenant farm women living in thirteen Piedmont counties, which comprise the subregional laboratory described in Part III. These women, in turn, are compared with an equal number from what is called the Deep South—Georgia, Alabama, Mississippi, and Louisiana.

While the focus of interest throughout the book is upon the mothers themselves, it is not possible to isolate them from their living environment on the farm. Although the lives of most women are somewhat affected by the occupations of their husbands, there is probably no group where the influence is more profound than in the case of tenant farm women. In the first place, they usually share the occupation; hence the type of farming determines whether they will spend a considerable part of the year in chopping, hoeing, and picking cotton or in planting, suckering, worming, "saving," and "stripping" tobacco. Then the farm which the tenant husband is able to rent prescribes their location, which, in turn, determines neighbors, schools, and churches. The farm obtained also provides their house, the physical plant for homemaking. The rental and credit practices, the season and the market, and the soil and method of farming determine the family income, while finally, the landlord-tenant relations and the local traditions set certain limits to social recognition and prestige attainable in a given neighborhood.

Thus, inasmuch as a knowledge of the farms is prerequisite

to an understanding of the women living on them, Part I is concerned with supplying such knowledge. Of course there is no one type of tenant farm or of tenant farm family. Even in an area delineated on the basis of internal homogeneity there are many gradations of farming and of farm people. Yet there are certain common features of tenancy in the Piedmont South which will be illustrated with groups of sketches of tenant farms and their families.

Some of the elements almost universally present, in the pattern of Southern farm tenancy, may be found in these sketches. There is the mining type of agriculture fostered by the single cash crop system which results in ever poorer land and insufficient production of food and feedstuffs. There is that nexus of factors—the world market, the share of the national income accruing to agriculture as a division of production, the distribution of this share between landlords and tenants, and the high cost of credit for financing farm operations—which results in a low income, inadequate diet and housing, and concomitant conditions of a depressed level of living for tenant farm families. And there is the relative lack of opportunity to rise in the economic scale, which results in depriving this group of any avenue for achieving the physical and spiritual goals of American democracy.

The sketches of farms and their families illustrate all these elements of the pattern of tenancy in combination with various modifications. They attempt to show the actual operation of the factors in order to suggest their meaning in the lives and work of tenant families. Finally, they serve to introduce the tenants themselves in their actual settings and to intimate what sort of people Southern tenant farms create and sustain.

Chapter 2

Of the Single Cash Crop System

THE PRODUCTION of cotton and tobacco has been the economic base of the South since colonial times. Yet these commodities have been labeled two of the South's greatest liabilities because of the type of agricultural economy they have fostered. When a farmer spends so much of his time on one of these crops that he cannot raise his food and feed, when he plants one of them consecutively without crop rotation and exhausts the soil, when he stakes his all on one crop which may in any year fail to yield a living income, the single cash crop system is at its worst.

In the Piedmont section of North Carolina, although the system is widespread, fortunately it does not exist in its most exaggerated form. There are several reasons why the extreme pathologies are not present. Excessively large plantations are rare in this group of counties. A relative lack of wealth concentration was to be found in the State even in pre-Civil War days. North Carolina's predominance of yeomen and scarcity of great estates have long been regarded with a certain degree of scorn by her more aristocratic neighbors to the north and to the south. Explaining the differences in the development of the economy would involve a consideration of causal historical factors, such as the nature of the original land grants and the type of settlers, which are beyond the scope of this study. Our concern is rather with the results observable in the present setup.

North Carolina and parts of Virginia have escaped the extreme waste of land associated with prolonged plantation economy. There is a deplorable amount of erosion, yet less than in the other states of the Southeast. On the other hand, the land is not so extremely fertile that there is such great pressure, as in the rich Delta, to put every acre of it into the money crop. Another factor making for availability of land for garden and feedstuffs on the tobacco farms is that because of the intensiveness of tobacco culture, only a small number of acres can be raised by one family. Moreover, usually only parts of the land in any one farm are suitable for tobacco since this crop has very exacting soil requirements.

On the sociological level, the smaller number of tenants per landlord has resulted in more personalized relations between the tenants and landlords than are found where great numbers of tenants are controlled by one man and harsh economic practices are routinized and applied automatically. In an area infiltrated with cotton mills, from which one might expect diffusion of ideas of unionism, the absence of any tenant farm union activity is evidence that class consciousness and the mobilization of resentment against landlords have not proceeded so far as in certain other parts of the South. This may also be partially explained by the fact that tenants on tobacco farms have not, as a rule, been reduced to the same degree of destitution as those in cotton areas, tobacco having been the more profitable crop in recent years.

And yet the evils of the cash crop system are clearly visible on most tenant farms in this area. Three farms are selected to illustrate phases of its inadequacy.

Farm One: A "No" Farm

In one of the counties containing these tenant farms there is not a single "yes" farm. This means that no farmer answered "yes" to the question of the Soil Conservation Bureau, "Do you produce any general farm products (those other than cotton or tobacco) above home consumption use?" Since only three farms report cotton, it is clear that here tobacco reigns supreme. Tobacco is the sole source of agricultural income on every farm. The stamp of its culture is evident to the most casual traveler, for in rural areas he cannot get out of sight of the sturdy, mud-chinked, log barns for curing. The habit of building of log often carries over to other structures, to stock barns and sometimes to houses. There is an absence of dairies, poultry buildings, cotton gins, grain mills, and of any other indication of diversified farming.

A diagonal divides the county into relatively good land on one side with a high percentage of Negroes and tenants, and poor land on the other with more whites and small owners. On the border line is a farm where the land is just fair—a little too strong for producing the best and most uniform quality of tobacco, with dark rather than light gray soil. It is owned by a county politician, who bought it cheaply three years ago at a foreclosure sale. At that time its only buildings were a two-room log house and two tobacco barns. This year he has added another room to the house, weatherboarded the two front rooms joined by a porch to the kitchen, rebuilt the front porch with substantial flooring and steps, and painted the front section white. The house, only a few hundred yards from a cross-roads country store, now presents such a respectable mien to the highway that one would hardly guess it to be the abode of a sharecropper.

If, however, a visitor enters the front door which opens into the sitting-bedroom, he will find the interior incongruous with the prosperous look of the gleaming white exterior. The floor slopes so badly that boards six inches high are propped under one end of the bed to level it off. Paper is tacked on parts of the walls, but crumbling mud spills from between the old logs of the exposed portion. Two beds and two chairs are all the furniture and three sick children lie in one of the beds. The mother explains that they all have colds, that one is just recovering from pneumonia. This winter has been hard on their health because they have not been able to shut out the wind with the repair to the house going on. They have continually had to breathe dust because the hammering knocks dirt out of the wall. She hates to think of what the doctor bill will be next fall although they waited until the child actually had pneumonia to call him.

Although the family have lived on this farm only a year, they have been in the neighborhood most of their lives. Once the husband got disgusted with farming because he seemed to run into debt more every fall. He tried mill work, but after being outdoors all his life he could not endure being shut up inside, and so he soon went back to farming. He prefers farming to anything else and the first thing he would do if he had some money would be to buy a piece of land of his own. But he is afraid he will never get it if things keep on the way they are.

He came out $30 "in the hole" this year. With the assistance of his wife and five children, he raised a crop of thirty-five thousand hills of tobacco (about eight acres) but it turned out badly. The blue mold attacked his plants early and he had to get other plants from another county. Some of these were not suited to his soil and many replantings were necessary. Finally there were five different kinds of tobacco growing in one field. The uneven quality resulting from this mixture was one reason he received so little for his crop. Another was that his strong soil made big "thrivers" which always sell badly. One lot was so bad that it brought him only a dollar a hundred. He said he would never have graded, tied, and taken it to market if he had known that that was all it would bring. He still has over a thousand pounds of so poor a quality that it is not worth taking to town. He will use it for fertilizer—perhaps for turnips, since it makes Irish potatoes quite "rusty."

The sharecropper and his wife both wish now that they had spent more of their time on food and less on tobacco. For instance, the tomatoes were ripe just when the crop had to be housed and the mother could not be spared from stringing tobacco leaves to can any for the winter. They had some wheat but not enough to last them through the year. The custom is to plant wheat only where tobacco has been the year before and the man who "tended" the land the preceding year had planted very few acres of tobacco. The sharecropper thinks "it's too bad that wheat gets harvested in the summer and you use up your wheat bran to feed the cow when she could be getting grass." Now they have nothing left to feed the cow, which has gone dry by this time. They will get half of the thirty-five barrels of corn they raised, but it will not be enough for meal, chickens, and as many hogs as they would like to have.

In spite of always giving first consideration to tobacco, they produced enough of their own food that their grocery bill for a family of eight was only $40 for the whole year. This was charged down at the crossroads store and paid in full when the crop was sold. The landlord had attended to buying the fertilizer, which practice they like better than going to the trouble of getting a government loan as they had to do the year before. The landlord had also furnished them with whatever cash they asked for and had been willing for them to pay off the store first and stay $30 in debt to him till next year. They think it is better to owe only one man "because then if you don't come out even he can't feel hard at you if you pay him all you have."

They will not have any more money until fall except what they ask the landlord for after the crop gets started. The only thing they bought last year besides groceries was clothes for the three children starting to school in September. Their oldest boy of thirteen is asking for a suit to wear to the State Capitol next month when the principal of the school takes the eighth grade for a trip, but they have told him there is no money and he will either have to wear overalls or not go. The wife has stopped going to church because she has not had a new dress in two years; they both agree that the main thing she is quarrelsome about is not having anything and "forever having to do without."

The greatest single factor in determining what these tenants will have at the end of the year is the number of pounds of tobacco they produce. This in turn is a function of the number of acres they plant. Hence the chief focus of conversation (as on all tobacco farms in March 1938) is the tobacco acreage allotments, which are made by a county committee of leading farmers working with the county agent. This sharecropper is pessimistic over the prospect of getting a just allotment. Allotments are made to the landowners rather than to the producing units, the families, and the owner can take what acreage he wants for himself and let the reduction, figured on a percentage basis for his entire holdings, be taken wholly out of the tenants' acreage. Two years ago this meant that both this sharecropper and his brother, who were farming together, got less than one and a half acres a family. This was not enough to keep them busy or to provide a living. At the same time their landlord kept for himself more acres than he could work. The sharecropper thinks that the only fair way to apportion it would be to allow the same acreage for each farming family, but he has little hope of this occurring.

The injection of this new element called acreage allotment into the accepted, traditional pattern has made this tenant aware not only of this particular unfairness, but also of other economic injustices he had formerly taken for granted. Where the cash crop means everything, the matter of acreage allotment administered by and to the advantage of the owners seems to be acting to produce class consciousness and resentment. The sharecropper broadened his observation and feelings on the allotment question into a generalization: "As long as the landlords are the ones to say who gets how many acres, the tenants will never get a square deal. Them that has can always fix it so the po' won't even have a chance to make anything."

Farm Two: An Indictment

In a corner of one county farthest removed from its industrialized seat of government lies "Harper's Old Field." It stretches from the crest of a long hill, topped by a freshly painted white chapel, for nearly a mile over rolling, good tobacco land. Families living in four of the five houses on the field bear the same name, as do the chapel, the "community," and many other families in this section of the county. Nearest the church is a modest home owned by an older member of this clan. Up the next small rise a crossroads leads on the left to a nonclan family's rather neat-looking tenant home, and on the right to houses of brothers who work on fourths some of their father's land, although the father's home is beyond the bounds of the field. Farther on and farther down is the last house, two rooms and a kitchen, almost falling down, unpainted, and unscreened, where lives a tenant farm mother with her husband and their ten surviving children.

One may now drive through this section with no more danger to be feared than muddying up his car—for the soil is redder than usual in tobacco areas. It was a different matter a decade ago in the heyday of prohibition, when certain members of the clan engaged in bootlegging and all the other members shared their suspicion of strangers. The hostility to strangers did not keep out a preacher who finally converted the oldest and wealthiest member. The old man burnt all his stills, stopped whiskey making in the community, and salved his conscience by spending several thousands of his illegal earnings to build the chapel which overlooks the field. The earlier religious enthusiasm has waned, but the chapel is truly a people's institution—three of the stewards can neither read nor write, for this clan has never held much with education.

A visitor will always find the tenant mother of the last house at home, for she has not left the immediate neighborhood in a good many years except to go to funerals. But she will not be found in the house unless the call is before breakfast, after supper, or on Sunday. "Gimme the field every time and tobacco growing—" she says, and she has enough children to be able to indulge her preference in tasks. She will be in the field, barn, or striphouse nearly twelve months a year. Two weeks after they stripped the last tobacco of one season, they were beginning the next year's crop—sowing the plant bed, "whupping" the seeds in with brush brooms, and covering the bed with cloth. On this bleak January day they had to stop raking every now and then and thaw their feet over a small fire, near which a younger child kept watch over a pint milk bottle full of tobacco seeds saved from last year's crop. This one pint of seeds will supply what plants they need for their ten acres of tobacco and will also furnish several neighbors who came to borrow that very morning.

The family farms fifty-nine acres of Harper's Old Field. Six adults do full-time fieldwork and five other members of the family help when the crop is being housed or when emergencies arise. Tobacco is the only money crop—the only farm commodity sold. However, the tenants raise corn enough for their two mules and for meal for themselves, wheat enough to supply their flour, field peas, sweet potatoes, and popcorn. They killed four hogs this winter and have five pigs saved for next year. They get about as much milk as they want from their cow, fed mainly on pea vines and grazed on land "laying out." They try to buy as little in the way of groceries as they can—just coffee, sugar, soda, and the like—but the mother says, "the way the beetles have ruint all the beans and the rest of the garden these last few years sure makes it harder to scrape up somp'n for a meal three times a day."

The mother, father, three grown sons, and a half-grown boy work in the field regularly; three other children go to school in the winter and help in the field in summer; the oldest daughter cooks and the next oldest constantly "tends" the ruptured baby boy of four. It is a simple matter to make an inventory of the economic returns of this family of twelve for a year. They were housed—the twelve slept in two rooms with four beds, they ate in a "shed kitchen," and in summer they sat on a rotting porch flush with the ground and half covered with mud washed on it from the slope up to the road. They were clothed—the men and boys in overalls which the mother always had to start patching after continued wear of a month or two, the girls and mother in homemade cotton dresses. They were fed—although undernourishment might be guessed from the fact that the twenty-one-year-old girl looked fourteen, the fourteen-year-old boy ten, the ten-year-old girl six, and so on all the way down. They had medical attention—chiefly from a "pellagra specialist," who is reputed to treat pellagra with a weak solution of hydrochloric acid. They claim this doctor saved the baby boy by warning them not to keep taking him to the city hospital for treatment because "the hospital doctors try out all their new things on people who go to clinics and are likely to kill you."

Their tobacco money was the family's sole source of cash. To the landowner they pay one-fourth of this money as well as one-fourth of the products other than tobacco. Within the family there is a further division. The mother gets all except the landlord's fourth from her tobacco patch, which brought over a hundred dollars this year. This fall all of her money went to pay for the burying of her last baby, who had died the year before, and to make a down payment of $40 on a new cook stove. She even had to get her husband to buy her some cloth to make a dress, although she is supposed to buy her own and her younger children's clothes from her patch sales. The three older boys are likewise allowed the proceeds of a patch, which they share with the two older sisters for cooking and keeping house and especially for taking care of their bird dog, their most prized possession. This year, however, the debts for fertilizer and for the groceries and clothes charged at the store amounted to more than all the father's remainder (after the proceeds from the two patches were deducted) and he could not let the children have all the money from their patch. He took enough to finish paying his debt at the store and let them have the remainder without keeping back any money to run on for the year. The boys found that the amount they had would exactly make a first payment on a second-hand truck. And so New Year's day found them with about $150 equity in a stove and truck as the only accumulations for the year, already charging whatever they got in the way of food or clothes until tobacco sales start in the fall. The boys hoped to do enough hauling for neighbors to pay for gasoline. Such are the yields extracted by six full-time and five part-time workers from this farm, which is called "good tobacco land," in a "pretty good" year.

In this particular case we may examine as possible factors making for the insufficiency of human needs the land, the market, the people, their folkways, and the "system." The farm shows none of the conspicuous effects of erosion such as gulleys or washes. The land is still "holding up" to the extent that the same plot can be used for tobacco for two successive years with no increase in amount of fertilizer used and no decrease in yield. The mother's patch on the red soil side of the road did not come up to expectation this year but the quantity and quality of tobacco from the whole ten acres planted were better than in most years. The family was allotted twelve acres but ten is as much as they can cultivate. Prices were fairly good, as tobacco prices go, and except for the beetles' destroying a considerable amount of the garden, there were no calamitous visitations.

For the people we have no such exact measuring units as dollars or pounds. The clan to which this family belongs has lived in this community for generations. A little twelve-year-old girl who is their cousin lives two miles away on a place her great-great-grandfather sold to a wealthier neighbor. He moved away but left a daughter and son-in-law, the little girl's great-grandmother and great-grandfather, as tenants for the new owner. Their son, her grandfather, lived there all his life as a tenant and now his widow and five of his children, one of them the little girl's mother, are still there. At the present there are seventeen children of the fifth generation living on this place and of the fourth generation of tenancy. Another member of the same clan and name who is more prosperous owns considerable holdings and has five tenants of his own name on his land, two of them his sons. The couple in the last house have lived there nine years and in another house a few miles away during the preceding years of their married life. One may say this clan exhibits stabilization of location, with a concomitant frequency of intermarriage between cousins. And yet the evidences of care and conservation of land which might be expected from long tenure of one family are missing. There are no terraces on the slopes, stumps show the yearly inroads upon the woods on the hill to supply the wood for curing the tobacco each year, while the line of plant beds encroaches a little farther every winter upon this no man's land of stumps. Weeds along the edges of fields and in the front yard may prevent washing, but they give the place an unkempt appearance. There are no fenced pastures. Instead there is a down-at-heel look resulting from certain land lying fallow and attention being lavished upon only the money crop. As the mother warmed her stockingless feet and legs she explained the numerous processes they were performing to prepare the seed bed for tobacco and observed, "I tell 'em if we was to spend even half as much time fixin' up a garden this size it would raise more vegetables than I could cook in a year."

Lack of education explains some of the ignorance and susceptibility to exploitation of this family. Neither mother nor father ever attended a day of school and neither can read or write. Of their twelve children only two have gotten so far as "stopping out in the fourth." Superstitious beliefs are numerous: the mother had insisted that they carry by hand the materials to the plant bed that morning and had taken the heaviest load herself, for she had dreamed the night before of her boys' being injured in the new truck and was determined that it should not leave the yard that day. A fortune teller had stopped by a few weeks before and had told the father that some one had placed a spell on him which only she could remove and which she did not because they had already spent all their tobacco money. He has felt pretty bad since then and has fainted once and is worried about it. The mother is glad they could not pay her to tell them any more, though, because she told them enough bad news without being paid anything. The buying judgment they exercise is often poor. The father has two good mules but they are no better than the two he had five years ago although he has swapped twice since then, paying as much as $100 to boot one fall when the horse trader brought out from town a sleekly groomed pair with red decorations around their necks. As the mother never has been able to buy anything except on time, she does not worry now when she finds that the stove she is paying $120 for in installments could have been bought for $70 cash. It really does not make any difference to her that cash prices are cheaper because she had only $40 and could not have got the other $30.

Modification of traditional folkways toward modern ideals of efficiency seems to be occurring only, or chiefly, in those aspects of life and work most directly related to the production of tobacco. Tobacco is what brings in the money and no effort is spared to try in the best ways known to make it bring in the most. The tobacco barns and striphouse are in better repair than the house, there is a more up-to-date and adequate supply of farming tools than of household appliances, there are two mules and they are better looked after than the one cow, and the boys' excuse for the latest acquisition is that they can haul tobacco to market in their truck. Of course, the accepted mode of tobacco culture seems anachronous in the twentieth century, with its requirement of innumerable hand operations, which would require considerable space for listing and a glossary for understanding. And yet there is a regularity and orderliness of accomplishing these akin to efficiency, which are not apparent in the other phases of farm and house work.

In summarizing this tenant farm we may recapitulate: its assets are good land, a good-selling money crop, an abundant and "docile" labor supply, and nonmobile operators; its liabilities are the lack of education, training, and buying experience of its tenants. From balancing these on paper we should expect the assets to outweigh the liabilities sufficiently for the results to be a reasonably decent level of living. From observation we find that minimum standards of adequacy are not even approached. The last family on Harper's Old Field scores an indictment against the "system."

Farm Three: A Foreclosed Home Place

Substantial, two-story, painted farmhouses are not uncommon in Oak Ridge vicinity, but one cannot learn the names of their dwellers in the county seat twelve miles south. These houses and their farms were mortgaged during the twenties by overambitious owners desiring more and more land. In the early thirties they became the property of land banks, insurance companies, and of various agencies and individuals who had made the loans. Of the original owners, only a doctor, who did not have to rely solely upon tobacco in the "bad" years of '32 and '33, has retained his home and farms. The others have disappeared and the home places are now identified by the names of their absentee owners, since the tenants shift too often for townspeople to keep track of their locations.

The most pretentious of these tenant-inhabited mansions has fluted columns and a wrought-iron fence around the yard in almost the grand manner. Most surprising, however, is its fresh coat of white paint set off by a background of trees and neatly creosoted outhouses. For when this house was surrendered by a member of one of the State's most prominent families in legal and political circles, it became the property of one of the Nation's largest insurance companies, whose policy is to preserve and keep up at least the outward appearance of its possessions. An overseer who supervises a great number of company-owned farms in seventeen counties has orders to keep the exteriors above reproach.

On closer inspection of the house and farm one begins to have doubts about the inside of the cup. Of the two hundred acres, less than fifty are now under cultivation. Some of the remainder is in woods, some of it is in pasture, but most of it, the present tenant claims, is "just plum wore out." With a Negro subtenant and his own family, he raised over fifteen acres of tobacco this year. That was planted on the very best of the remaining land and was fertilized heavily but the yield was poor. He did not come out even this year; he still owes his doctor bill and a good bit more to the insurance company. It not only advanced him the fertilizer, but from March through July supplied him $30 a month *cash* for his family to live and farm on. There is no landlord in the vicinity who has given out money like that—$150—since he can remember. His share of the crop was not enough to pay it all back, though, and worse than that, the insurance company sold the place last month to a man who lives in a nearby town and who will not be so free with money. The tenant is applying to the government for fertilizer loan and will buy clothes and groceries wherever he can get credit.

This family, too, could have raised more of what they will need to eat if they had not spent all their time on tobacco. They did raise enough corn and wheat but no "patches." The mother put up over four hundred quarts of vegetables and fruit last summer and raised enough "snap" beans to sell a few in the nearest mill town. The proceeds from this were their only income during the year other than from tobacco. They killed four hogs, which will be meat enough to last till next fall, but the mother feels they could have raised much more of such produce as sweet potatoes, field peas, and cane for syrup, if they had not given so much of their time to the money crop. She thinks that even the land with the bad gullies and washes in it would have grown watermelons and cantaloupes.

Because they thought they were going to move this year they did not sow any wheat in the fall. "That's just one of the bad things about tending land and never knowing how long you're going to stay. What's worse is letting the land go. If you plant rye on the land that's been used for tobacco one year you can use it over and over again. But you can't blame 'attendants' for not doing that—specially when we thought we was going to move Christmas. The folks before us didn't do anything either and that's why we want to go somewhere else—the land's got so bad you can't make anything off'n it. Renters don't take care of the land because it ain't theirs and they don't know when they'll be leaving; and landlords don't fix up the inside of the house because they don't have to live there and nobody sees it."

With this remark the mother exhibited the part of the nine-room house in which they live. Because unlike most tenants they have closets, there was not the usual array of clothing hanging on the walls. The bareness was accentuated by the scarcity of furniture. With only a bed and three straight chairs in the living room, the rain-stained wall paper peeling off and streaming down was the most conspicuous feature of the room. In the hall about half the plastering had fallen. The exposed laths and broken-out stair banisters seemed incongruous with the graceful columns visible through the glass-topped front door. While a rural line supplying electricity at a minimum rate of 78 cents a month passed through the front yard, the owners had not been willing to bear the expense of having the house wired. Smoke smudges indicated previous locations of kerosene lamps.

Here live the tenant, his wife, and nine of his children, ranging from two to sixteen years of age. His two oldest daughters, aged nineteen and twenty, married and moved away this year. Another child died three years ago. The wife is now carrying her thirteenth child, although this condition did not keep her from doing the largest part of grading the tobacco this fall. Her expressed attitudes toward her situation reveal some of the basic elements of tenant ideology and are clear from the following. She gets to feeling pretty bad when she's "that way" now, especially since she's had such a hard time with her last four—two doctors each time because they've had to take the babies ever since her twins were born. But she makes up her mind she just won't let it make her cross with her children the way some women are. And she remembers what the Bible says, "Be content with your lot," and tries to keep from worrying about not coming out even with the crop or about how they're going to feed and clothe another child. With thirteen children born in twenty-two years she has spent her life either being pregnant or having a baby too young to go anywhere. She gave up going to church long ago—or anywhere else. But she figures that you have to work and give all your time and energy to something, and she'd rather it would be to children than to anything else. Her two daughters who married this year never gave her a minute's worry and if she can just live to see them all grown and married she'll feel she's done a good work. In common with many, many other tenant mothers, however, she fervently hopes that this one on the way will be the last one.

The worst thing of all about having so many children has been that she can't give them what they want and need. Take her girls fifteen and sixteen, now, in high school and doing well in their books. One of them is on the basketball team and they're having a banquet for them this week. This morning she said she had to have 80 cents to pay her share of it or she couldn't go and the other one said she had to have a voile dress because she was supposed to be a waitress for the banquet. There was one dollar left in the house—they had saved a little when they sold the last tobacco to have something to spend on Christmas and this was the last of it. And so the mother gave them the dollar together and told them to do the best they could do with it and to have a good time because it would have to last till next fall. "That's what's the hardest thing of all—having fine children and not being able to spend on them what you see they need." Yet this was said in a cheerful tone with no trace of irritation as the two youngest children tugged at her dress and interrupted in one way or another. Her countenance became more grave as she generalized her experiences to sum up the conditions of her class: "Tenants ain't got no chance. I don't know who gets the money, but it ain't the poor. It gets worse every year—the land gets more wore out, the prices for tobacco gets lower, and everything you got to buy gets higher. Like I told you, I'm trying to 'be content' like the Bible says and not to worry, but I don't see no hope."

Chapter 3

Of the Decline of Cotton

SINCE 1920 the cotton growing sections of the Southeast have suffered heavily from the boll weevil, competition from the Southwest, a partial loss of the world market, and diminishing returns from impoverished soil. In a few very fertile areas—the Delta being the most important—cotton may still be produced at a profit. In others the introduction of subsidiary money crops such as peanuts, peppers, or livestock, has supplemented or entirely replaced the income from cotton. In many other places, however, where no substitute money crop has been successful, former cotton farmers are destitute.

The Piedmont area affords examples of the two latter situations. Where the land is suitable for tobacco, cotton has been largely displaced. This displacement has proceeded rather rapidly in spite of two retarding influences: the resistance of farm people to change from the sort of farming they have done since childhood, and the various quota and allotment restrictions made by the Department of Agriculture to prevent overproduction.

Where the soil is not the type required for tobacco, the decline in income from cotton has been more difficult to balance. In general, the level of living has been stringently reduced unless some sort of subsidy has been found. Wages from cotton, hosiery, and tobacco factories have provided cash for running expenses of cotton farm families fortunate enough to get one or more members jobs in the mills. Social security payments have made possible the continuance of cotton farming where eligibility for Old Age Assistance or Aid to Dependent Children could be established. Checks to mothers of boys in the Civilian Conservation Corps have paid fertilizer and grocery bills for many cotton farm families. When these special qualifications could not be met, work and direct relief have often subsidized cotton production. The rules of eligibility for WPA certification, however, make it very difficult for a farmer with any sort of a crop to be certified. Meager county budgets also limit direct relief in most cases to surplus commodities, sewing-room garments, and some medical aid. Even these are not available to farmers of industrial counties in times of strikes or heavy layoffs. This latter fact as presented by certain social workers to relief-seeking farmers makes for the development of an anti-labor-organization spirit among them.

Thus various economic adjustments to the decline of cotton with concomitant modifications in patterns of living are observable in the area chosen for study. Among the older generation there is almost always present a harking back to the Golden Age when cotton brought 40 cents a pound. But they no longer expect the era to return and disillusionment with farming is widespread. An evidence of this is their expressed desire that their children go into work other than farming, in spite of believing country life is the best, since "nobody can make a living off of cotton any more."

Farm Four: A Cotton Farm

Ten years ago the only tobacco growing in Owen community was in tiny patches for home chewing. Now tobacco barns dot the sandy, gray fields at frequent intervals, and the woods show marks of recent incursions for curing supplies. On the Mount Moriah Church road only one farm is left with no tobacco barns. For nearly a decade a couple have lived here and clung to cotton because "that's what we're used to." Tenants nearby have been forced to change over to the more remunerative tobacco by a landlord who owns most of the land around. But this family pay "standing" rent of nine hundred pounds of lint cotton to another smaller landowner, and with an autonomy not possible to sharecroppers, they may raise what they please.

Cotton has rewarded meagerly such constancy and loyalty to its cultivation. Things became so bad in the depression that this family faced one Christmas without a cent and had to sell their last four chickens to buy "fixings and Santa Claus." Their plight was in some ways worse than that of sharecroppers, who often had someone to furnish them. Finally the mother, a Home Demonstration Club member, was given a job helping other farm women with canning. Her work was highly commended by the county agent, for she went right to the homes of those who had not been willing to go to meetings because they had no stockings or decent clothes to wear. When this was over the agent was able to get the father WPA work driving a truck several days a week. Many debts had accumulated before this cash began to come in—fertilizer bill, back preacher's salary, and a heavy doctor bill incurred when the mother had pneumonia. But every second week when the pay check arrived they used a part of it to pay what they owed. The mother began to take butter, eggs, and canned goods to the curb market on Saturdays, the nearly-grown son started working one day a week at a filling station, and 1937 saw them out of debt.

Cotton prices were low that year. Of the eight bales they made on fourteen acres with one horse, two went for rent and all the rest for fertilizer. But they produced corn to feed the horse and chickens, "swapped in" the cottonseed for enough cottonseed meal to feed the cow a year, raised three hogs to supply themselves with meat, and sweet potatoes, peas, and vegetables for home use. By raising most of their food and by spending sparingly for clothes this family of five during the year saved just over $200 from the father's WPA wages of $56 a month.

On the last visit to this family the mother was beaming. Almost brimming over with news and excitement, she restrained herself while there was the customary exchange, demanded by courtesy, of reports on health, weather, children, and crops. Then she burst out, "We've bought us a home since you was here last," in a tone of justifiable pride. An old couple had died within the year and their three-room house with its two acres of land had to be put on sale that the "heirers" might divide the property. Her husband heard that one of them had bid it in at $200 and after a family consultation he went and raised the bid to $220. Being determined to pay cash, when they found the family's combined resources to the last penny were eight dollars short of the amount bid, the mother hastened to collect things for the curb market. There she made the balance and enough more to pay the fees for legal services when they actually had the deed made out.

The $220 house and lot were a mile away. Sitting back two hundred yards from the highway between a tall group of pines and a neighbor's field, it did not look particularly bad from a distance, for the front had once been painted white. Close-at-hand inspection revealed broken steps, only one window in each of the three rooms, and an unceiled kitchen. Accustomed to such minor deficiencies from having lived in tenant homes all her life, the mother was not the least dismayed by these, but instead was inordinately elated upon discovering that the house was wired for electricity from the rural electrification line passing along the highway.

They will raise cotton one more year, although it does no more than get the farm rent paid for them. From other income they will save enough to get their new house fixed up so that they can move in and give up cotton forever. There is land enough for garden and patches and they will rent a few acres of corn land from a neighbor. Assuming the continuation of WPA employment, they will get along as well financially without farming, the burden of which has been upon the mother and children since the father started driving the truck.

This couple had looked toward home and farm ownership ever since they were married twenty-four years ago. During the first ten years they were never able to get ahead because they farmed with the husband's father, a tenant, moving wherever he moved, living in whatever sort of second house was available. They had no team and therefore their share of the crop was only one-half. The husband had to spend so much time helping his aging father that he couldn't "tend" much land for himself. But during this period they began planning to improve their status. After two children were born in the first three years of their married life, they decided to try not to have any more because the expense of children would keep them from getting ahead. An old "granny" woman advised the mother to practise *coitus interruptus*, which they have used as a method of birth control for twenty years now. Only two more children have been born in this time—an evidence of strength of resolve and purpose. For a few years after the husband's father died they were able to save a little each year —just enough to keep them hoping—but the depression wiped out this accumulation. Their economic history has been related from that time.

This example of the results of cotton farming is condemnatory. Here was a family of two parents and four children with good health, with a love of farming and fieldwork, with demonstrated thrift, with self-restraint and temperance, with high motivation toward achieving ownership—and yet the results of their efforts on the cotton farm were complete impoverishment, from which they were rescued only by work relief.

Farm Five: A Small Owner

In the conventional hierarchy of status, the tenant farmer is bounded below by the wage laborer and above by the small owner operator. Flexibility of boundary lines permits of intermediate grades such as part owners and wage hands who also "tend a little land." In spite of the difficulties of "climbing," there is still a residuum of vertical mobility in both directions. Hence it is not out of place in a treatment of tenancy to present an adjacent type of farmer to illustrate both similarities and differences.

The farm to be described is in an area where small owners are more common than tenants. It is in a school district which extends about five miles in each direction from a central village. Although the village contains about a thousand people, it is not a trading center but predominantly a residential suburb of a city nearly ten miles away. Laborers and poorly paid white collar workers find living in the country and commuting cheaper than living in town. Each automobile owner has his gasoline expenses shared by the four or five people who ride to town and back with him daily. Some of them own homes in the village or open country and often their families do part-time farming. Others rent houses with or without attached farms along or near the highway bisecting the district.

North of the highway the slopes are steep and the hills high. The red clay soil has fared badly under continuous cotton cultivation. One field has had cotton raised on it by the same family for over a hundred years. Erosion has progressed so far that a large tract is being bought up, evacuated, and retired from farming by the National Park Commission. A map of the project shows that the area was made up of many small tracts, few of which were large enough to have on them a family other than that of the owner operator. Of the families moved off only two accepted the proffered services of the Farm Security Administration for rehabilitation elsewhere, since these independent owners felt capable of and preferred managing their own affairs. A few people who had lived here all their lives objected to moving, but most of them had come out so badly against the ravages of the boll weevil and erosion during the last few years that they were glad enough to move away.

South of the highway the soil is also red but the fields are more level. The land is suited for neither tobacco nor truck farming, which would be desirable because of nearness to the city, because with its topsoil long gone it is too tight and heavy. Enterprising teachers of agriculture have stimulated poultry raising and there are two small dairies, but these have never become adequate substitutes for cotton in providing cash income, and most of the families send one or more members to town to work. Here, also, holdings are small; there are no old plantation homes or visible signs of former large estates.

Where two country roads cross several miles below the village, an unpainted, five-room house stands opposite a small church. Its kitchen was a one-room house eleven years ago when the present owner purchased for $2,600 the fifty-two acres which go with it. He and his wife had farmed as tenants for the first nineteen years of their married life on her father's place a mile away. They saved enough to make a down payment on this land and to buy lumber for building additional rooms to the house. This latter expenditure was a necessity since when they moved, the mother at the age of thirty-five had already borne eleven children.

Only twelve of the fifty-two acres were cleared when the

land was purchased and these have been gradually increased to thirty-seven. The fields are quite rocky but in good years have yielded better than a bale of cotton to the acre. Cotton has been the only money crop except for a few surplus vegetables sold irregularly during the summer. The farmer has usually had about twelve acres in cotton and has used the rest for food and feed crops, producing enough for his two mules, two cows, a few hogs, and chickens. His wife has a garden from which each year she puts up enough canned vegetables to last through the winter, and their small apple and peach orchard has begun bearing enough for home use in the last two years.

They were able to meet the payments on the farm for a few years, although the deaths of two children preceded by long illnesses meant heavy expenses as did the two more babies who took the places of the lost ones. Then several years of severe boll weevil infestation and low prices for cotton made them unable to meet even the interest payments and their mortgage was foreclosed. After farming on an uncertain pseudo-tenant basis for a year the farmer was able to get a loan through a government land bank to buy back his farm for $2,000. He says the government is the best place to owe money to, because it charges only five and one-half percent interest and will not so quickly close one out although it will take the farm finally if the farmer doesn't pay.

In the fall of 1937 the paying even of interest was impossible. From eleven acres of cotton he made only six bales because the weevil was extra bad. When he sold this at seven and one-half cents a pound the proceeds paid the fertilizer bill with exactly $9.58 left over. The four older children who had left home were all married with their own financial responsibilities and could not help out. The situation became more desperate, not only from fear of foreclosure, but also from need of money for living expenses for a family of nine still at home with six children in school. The farmer looked for a job in the city but none was to be had. Finally he was allowed forty hours a week work on a roadway beautification project, but bad weather during the fall has kept him from ever making full time. Nevertheless, this cash from work relief has prevented or postponed a complete financial collapse.

Badly though he needed the money, in February 1938 he was planning to give up the job soon to get his crop planted. Yet he could not make definite plans for his planting because of the delay of the crop control referendum. He thought about two acres of his land would be suitable for tobacco and wanted to try raising it, but was afraid there would be no quotas to spare for new tobacco growers. He was going to ask for an allotment nevertheless, since he said the county agent can sometimes increase one thing or another—although it makes those who ask for increases and do not get them "powerful mad" when he gives them to others. He was afraid, though, that they would allow him just the eleven acres of cotton again. When asked if he would plant these eleven acres if he knew ahead of time that the boll weevil would be as bad as it was the preceding year, and that he would come out with only nine dollars for his year's work, the farmer paused for a moment and while thinking seemed suddenly to become aware of the futility of his efforts and enraged over it. "No, I wouldn't," he declared defiantly, but he had no answer to his wife's, "Well, what *would* you do?" Reminded of the inescapability of his dilemma, he retreated from his stand and covered his outburst of aggression with a typical statement of the optimistic philosophy which ever sustains farmers, "Well, we always keep hoping that the next year will turn out better."

With cash income so low and ownership itself so precarious, there are yet differentiae advantageous to the owner farmer as compared with the tenant. In years when there has been a bit to spare he has spent it on minor improvements to his house. These improvements have resulted in a more livable home than most tenant homes. He is now enjoying fruits from an orchard which a tenant could never have planted with any assurance of being at the same place when it began to bear. Although last year he had to sell one of his two cows to pay a hospital bill and although his brood sow with a litter of ten pigs died, he still has a better supply of livestock than the modal tenant. As a landowner he enjoys more prestige in the community, his children do not have to change from school to school, and he boasted of knowing everybody in the nearby village until a few years ago when more "town people" moved out. Yet along with the tenant he faces the common plight of those engaged in agricultural labor—inadequate returns for productive labor. WPA has prolonged his owner's status, but he does not know how long the work will last. He wants to make the most out of it he can while it does. Somewhat resigned to the dictates of the weather from long years of farming, he could not restrain murmurs of impatience at the rain beating on the kitchen window, since now it kept him from a day's pay in cash.

Farm Six: SUBSIDIZED SHARECROPPING

In some localities of the Subregion it is almost impossible to find a white sharecropper family living entirely on proceeds from farming on halves. In cotton growing areas especially is this true, for the returns have been so low in recent years that often even a subsistence level of living is maintained only by some of the forms of subsidy mentioned above. On one farm visited the inadequate income from cotton has been supplemented for several years by raising a small amount of tobacco, and, in addition for nearly a year now, by an Aid to

Dependent Children monthly payment. A brief history of the family illustrates ascent and descent of the tenure ladder as well as the necessity of subsidy.

The widowed mother of this family was the daughter of a small owner in a nearby county, whose farm had been a wedding present from his father-in-law. She was one of eleven children, all of whom worked on their parents' farm, and was considered her father's best "hand" when she married at the age of twenty-four. The man she married was nine years older, for as a tenant's son he had resolved to wait to marry until he had saved enough to buy himself a farm. He bought and paid for a thirty-one-acre farm before marrying and with his wife lived on it for twenty years growing cotton. It was well that the farm was paid for in advance, for during the twenty years nine children were born to them and no savings were accumulated.

About the time of the birth of her last child the mother began to notice peculiarities of behavior in her husband but did nothing about them for a year. During that year he lost his mind, but while he was still managing his affairs he mortgaged his farm and disposed of the money no one knows how. In another year he died leaving his family absolutely nothing except the home furnishings. With the oldest son of twenty-one as the head of the family, the mother and children began sharecropping. In the nine years since the father's death, four sons one by one have succeeded to the headship of the family as the oldest ones married and moved away to farm separately. The diminishing labor force has brought in a decreasing income. This year with the mother at fifty-five no longer physically able to do field work and with three of the four remaining children at home attending school, they have been cut from a two-horse to a one-horse farm and they expect even smaller acreage next fall. Never in the nine years have they come out far enough ahead to pay the $142 owed on the father's burying expenses or to purchase a team and implements to elevate their tenure status. Three years ago they moved to the present county because the oldest son at home married a girl who wanted to live near her own people. This son has moved away, but the family remain, now headed by a twenty-year-old boy. They have fared worse in this second county for the land is of a poorer quality.

Their landlord allowed them $10 a month "furnish" after May last year, but in the preceding months they were wholly dependent upon a newly granted ADC allowance. Even with this subsidy they did not come out even at settling time last fall. The mother is of the old school, who think it not a woman's place to "tote the pocketbook," and considers it the greatest good fortune of her widowhood that she has always had at home a son old enough to manage the financial arrangements of the farm. Even so, she has her own ideas about why they have done so badly and she expresses them with considerable bitterness. First, prices aren't right—the five bales of cotton they made brought less than $100 and their tobacco not that much. Then they had to pay too much for fertilizer because the credit prices are too high and, "When the landlord just sends it out and collects from you at the end of the year you don't know what you're paying for. But if you don't have some money saved up so you can pay cash in the spring there's just nothing to do about it. And it goes mighty hard to see everything you've worked for all year go to pay fertilizer bills before you ever see any of it." The mother is "down in her back" still from picking cotton and doing all the grading of the tobacco, but her resentment is directed toward the lack of money returns rather than toward the impairment to her health.

The children with only sharecropper status are getting

much more education than their mother, an owner's daughter, did a generation ago. She went only three months a year for several years to an ungraded, one-room, one-teacher school and doesn't know how to estimate what grade she reached. Her children have all gone as far as the fifth grade before stopping and two have gone as far as the eighth. Of those at home now, the eleven-year-old boy is in the fifth grade, the fourteen-year-old boy in the seventh, and the seventeen-year-old girl in the ninth. The retardation progressing with age is partially explainable on the basis of the cumulative effect of starting late and stopping early each year. Except for the youngest all the children have failed to make a grade once or twice because of staying out to help with the farming. They have usually had to stay out till the cotton was picked and the tobacco stripped in the fall. They have never complained about what they have had to do for the family and the mother thinks she has certainly been blessed with dutiful children. The boys in turn have worked as hard as her husband ever did to provide for the younger children; the seventeen-year-old girl does all the milking, washing dishes, and making beds even while she is going to school.

What worries the mother about the younger children is the notions they get in their heads at the consolidated school. They go on a bus and don't get home until late in the "evening" and yet they won't take a lunch to school now unless it's sandwiches made of bought "loaf bread." Even at home they will not eat "plain bread" (corn bread) any longer, but have to have flour biscuits at every meal. She always has something saved for them from dinner—which has to be in the middle of the day when there is a man working—and they eat when they get home from school. The family could get along with spending very little on groceries if the children would eat corn bread, because they raise enough corn for meal. This year they killed their own hogs but the beetle kept them from canning any vegetables and they have no fruit trees on the place. The children like milk but the cow does not give much now because they have no feed for her except corn shucks and meal and cannot afford to buy any.

In spite of certain grievances this mother faces her situation rather placidly now because of the security the Aid to Dependent Children monthly checks afford. She says the landlord didn't give them half of the soil conservation check and she guesses he will do the same with the money for acreage reduction, but he doesn't get his hands on the check from the "Welfare." Small as it is, this constitutes the first regular cash income she has ever had and it brings her a tremendous relief from worry. She supposes they will keep on farming as long as there are enough children left, but thinks "it's good to know we'll have something to live off of besides cotton and tobacco."

Chapter 4

Of the Agricultural Ladder

THE CONCEPT of the agricultural ladder has long been one of the fundamental tenets of Americanism in rural life. It is the theory that any young man may start on the bottom rung as a wage laborer and, by industry and thrift, climb rung by rung through the stages of sharecropper, share tenant, cash renter, and part owner to the final, topmost rung of full-owner status. This concept guarantees opportunity to all—that economic and social classes are open, an essential of a functioning democracy.

There have been those, more frequently in the past than at present, who have climbed the ladder as the theory prescribes. Along with the granting of recognition to these successful ones has gone a tacit condemnation of those who have been unable to lift themselves from the lower rungs of the ladder. Failure has often been accounted for on biological or moral grounds, that is, sharecroppers remain sharecroppers because they are of bad hereditary stock, poor whites, or because they do not have the middle-class virtues of industry and thrift, or because they do not care enough to try to improve their status. Undoubtedly the extended agricultural depression has made climbing the ladder more difficult and less frequently achieved. This has led to a questioning of the traditional explanations of failure and to examination of both handicapping factors affecting the adequacy of the people, such as diet and social impoverishment, and external factors, such as the state of agriculture and the economic injustices of tenancy and its associated credit practices.

Here the dilemma of all qualitative population studies is

reached. In oversimplified terms there are the three variables: "quality" of people, their environment (in an inclusive sense), and their achievement. Since "quality" is the most elusive of measurement, estimates of it have to be inferred from approximate measures of the two others. The assumption that quality varies directly with achievement underlies the older biological and moral interpretations of failure to climb the ladder. Recognition of the importance of the whole range of environmental factors leads to a more valid but less conclusive interpretation. The specific question becomes, what degree of quality can we infer in people whose achievement as measured by position on the tenure ladder is low, but whose environment (including the handicapping and external factors mentioned above) has been very disadvantageous? Can the combination of many disadvantaging environmental factors account for the low level of achievement or must innate inferiority be posited? No conclusive answer can be given until scientific inquiry has developed more adequate measures of achievement and of environmental factors and has clarified the functional relationship between the three variables. Meanwhile, an agnostic point of view concerning quality seems logically inevitable and its adoption seems a distinct advance over older, dogmatic interpretations.

The content of this chapter merely points out some of the actual difficulties commonly encountered in climbing the ladder in order to suggest the importance of environmental considerations. Since full owners are not included in this study, complete success stories are automatically excluded. On the other hand, since most of the tenants visited were not in the process of climbing, and since almost any family in the other chapters can be taken to illustrate the case where difficulties are insuperable, a story of complete failure is also omitted. The illustrations are limited to two farmers who seem to be actually in the process of ascending the agricultural ladder, one by his own efforts and the other with the help of the Farm Security Administration.

Farm Seven: REMNANTS OF THE FRONTIER

There is a cared-for look to a tiny house sitting in the edge of pine woods a quarter of a mile off a highway through the cotton growing section of one of the counties. It is distinguished from the tenant houses nearby in not yet having become weathered—none of them is painted. When the woods were cleared, a few trees and saplings were left for shade and decoration. A new well and a new potato house adorn the back yard, and rocks picked up from the cotton field across the wagon road leading from the highway mark off a front yard in which dahlias and roses have been recently set out. In the windows are curtains made of flour sacks but embroidered by hand.

This home was built and is owned by a young tenant farmer who lives in it. He is still a tenant because after saving for nearly ten years he was able to make a down payment on only a narrow strip of five acres of woodland. The story of how he has cleared parts of this between busy seasons of field work on cotton and corn, of how he built unaided the three-room house upon it—"even the chimney," his wife boasts—is reminiscent of frontier accomplishments. Much of the furniture is also of his own handiwork since there has been no cash to spare for buying it. A homemade "kiddie-coop" has served for the last two of the six children this couple have had in their thirteen years of married life.

The part-owner rung of the ladder was not easily achieved by this couple. Until three years ago, when they bought the land their home is on, none of their children was old enough to be of much economic value in farming. The mother did almost full-time field work in addition to household duties up to the last minute of her "ever' two year" pregnancies and was back in the field again before the baby was a month old. For the last two years the oldest boy, who is now twelve but weighs less than ninety pounds, has done a full man's work, including plowing. The little fellow is proud of being regarded as a regular hand and is rewarded by being taken to cornshuckings in the neighborhood with his father. He likes everything except plowing in the new ground—the patches cleared on their own land—where the old roots catch onto the plow and are almost too much for his small weight to manage. The next three boys chop and pick cotton; none of them can begin school in the fall until the picking is finished.

They have their own mule now, but still have to pay one-fourth of their cotton and one-third of their corn to the landowner, even though they are not supplied with a house as in the customary arrangement. This year their share from eight acres of cotton was not sufficient to pay their year's debt for fertilizer and running expenses. These last were kept down to a minimum for this couple have their minds set on buying the twenty-five acres they "tend" now and they buy nothing they can do without in their attempt to save. The mother has not had a new pair of shoes in two years and her only pair is too worn out now to be resoled again, although she goes barefooted in the summer to save them. She has only one pair of hose and they are cotton. She saves them for Sundays and does without any leg protection while doing outdoor work in even the coldest weather. When she was forced to go to the hospital for a difficult instrumental delivery of a baby last summer, she returned home the next day to save expense and to be with her children.

Her ingenuity with flour sacks is remarkable; from them

she has made not only the curtains but all of her pillowcases and most of the clothing for her two youngest children. She has found a place where one can buy rayon seconds very cheaply and the material for her homemade Sunday dress cost only forty cents. For every day she wears cotton dresses so old that no pattern or color is any longer discernible, and for warmth, an old, ragged, discarded coat of her husband's, which belonged to a suit he had before they were married. In the mornings her hair is often rolled up for she has not lost all thought of appearance at the age of thirty even though she has had nothing to spend on adornments. She would like to be able to buy some new clothes but she regrets more not having money to buy pencils and paper for her children in school. The teachers say they are getting along well and the oldest is leading the sixth grade in spite of being kept out to help with field work at least two months a year.

Although they have lived on almost nothing in the way of cash expenditures, they have been unable to pay anything on their six acres for the last two years. Yet their aim toward ownership has not swerved and they are pursuing it doggedly despite discouragements. Relying wholly on cotton for cash income, they have come to accept the boll weevil and market prices as beyond their control, but they cling to the idea that their hard work and economy will eventually gain for them their ends.

Farm Eight: A Prospective Tenant Purchaser

One county's complete dependence on agriculture as a source of income has necessitated so much state subsidy in education and other services that it has been dubbed a "pauper county" by residents of neighboring areas. There are no industries, unless two small sawmills be so classified, and no towns where some member of a rural family might have opportunity to supplement the farm income. The county seat is only a tiny village serving as a trading center for the impoverished countryside. Its courthouse looks desolate and deserted save when a farmers' meeting fills its halls, yards, and public square with bona fide "dirt" farmers vitally interested in crop control and acreage allotments.

Highways leading from the central village traverse varied topography and soil type—red, yellow, and several shades of gray may be showing in the same field. Certain characteristics, however, prevail rather uniformly: considerable erosion, telltale areas of broomstraw and scrub pine indicative of poor soil, and yet spots suitable for tobacco on almost every farm, and a preponderance of log construction in buildings.

A half mile back from one of the main roads through the hilly section is an old, unpretentious homestead on a two-hundred-acre farm. The six-room house is two-story, but its low ceilings and modest lines do not suggest plantation grandeur. Clumps of bulbs which have survived the rooting of pigs, a half dozen boxwoods in the front yard, and a family cemetery farther down the hill suggest the permanency of residence of its former owners, while a new barn and well-fenced stockyard show practices of its present tenant which are unusual in this one-cash-crop section.

A depression foreclosure transferred ownership from the third generation of the family whose name is on the hillside tombstones to an industrial magnate of the next county, who picked up a number of farm holdings at absurdly low prices. He has no liking for supervising tenants, however, and has agreed to sell the place at a reasonable figure to the present tenant if the latter can get the Farm Security Administration to make the loan for a tenant purchase. The limited appropriations make possible such a small number of these loans that competition is keen for them and a rigid scrutiny of the past farming record of the applicant is supplemented by a period of observation. This farmer is more or less on probation; his management and production this year will probably determine whether he will receive government aid in becoming an owner.

He has already progressed one rung of the ladder since the depression—or more strictly, two rungs up and one down. The years 1932 and 1933 convinced him that sharecropping was unbearable. At that time none of his children had left home, yet with their work, his wife's, and his own he went deeper in debt every year. He heard of a small place with about ten not very desirable, but still cultivable, acres which could be rented for $35 a year. He decided he would stake everything on an attempt to extricate himself from his hopeless situation. He possessed neither work animals, implements, nor the cash for rent. The only asset salvaged from years of working on halves was a flock of chickens. He sold these chickens for $10, which he paid down on the rent so that he could move to the new place. After his family had lived for quite a while on "flour and water gravy" he secured a $105 government loan to use in producing his crop. Before this loan came through the farmer insisted to neighbors, who were dubious of the outcome of his venture, that he would dig up the ten acres by hand with a mattock if he could not get a mule, rather than go back to sharecropping. When the money did come he used $10 of it to buy an old, feeble mule, a buggy, and a plow, and the remainder to "run" him until his tobacco was sold. His crop was no tremendous success for the land was quite poor and he had not been able to get all the fertilizer he needed, but it brought in enough to pay the balance of the rent, the government loan, to make a down payment on two good mules, and to purchase an adequate supply of farming implements.

This achievement in one year, when he had started from

scratch except for the ten dollars worth of chickens, brought the farmer favorable attention from the community. As a consequence he was offered the opportunity of share renting the place where he is now. Technically a step backwards, it was actually an improvement economically to change from cash renting a very poor and small farm to share renting one with better land and house and considerable pasture. In his three years' stay he has grown tobacco as his chief cash crop, but not to the exclusion of food, feed, and livestock. His wife boasts that this past year they have entirely "lived at home"—grown their own wheat, pigs, chickens, vegetables, and with proceeds from selling a few eggs and chickens have paid for the commodities they could not produce, such as sugar and coffee. Although her family of two sets of twins and seven single children was increased by a third set of twins this year, she has managed the poultry and canned enough to supply this large family through the winter, besides having helped with the stripping of the tobacco.

Their tobacco last fall sold for almost exactly $1,000, of which $250 went to the landlord. A mistake in buying judgment, frankly admitted by the tenant, made him lose a large part of the $750 he should have cleared. His zeal for increasing his livestock capital—now six cows and about twenty pigs—outran his corn supply, since the previous year had been very dry and the corn crop short. When his own feed was exhausted he made weekly orders from a man who delivered by truck to his barn door without making too careful inquiry into prices. When the bill of several hundred dollars was presented at settling time in the fall he was floored by the amount. Since he has been endeavoring to increase the number of his stock, he sold so few of them during the year that his share of their sales proceeds came nowhere near meeting the feed bill and he had to draw heavily on his tobacco money for the purpose. He is sure, however, that his good corn yield last year will prevent this occurring during the coming year.

This couple faces the year hopefully. If the tenant purchase loan is made they have already planned exactly how they will manage so as to be able to pay the purchase price in full within six years. They plan to sell part of the timber, but they will not sell the boxwood at any price because it is "a part of the place" which they are already thinking of as their own. This couple's attitude of partnership and far more equalitarian relationship than is common are evident in their joint accounts of past farming experiences and plans for the future. They are rather confidently now waiting on Washington.

Chapter 5

Of Modifications of the Pattern

IT IS TRUE that certain features of tenancy illustrated prevail rather uniformly through the Piedmont South. On the other hand, some of the most interesting tenant farms from a sociological point of view are those which show modifications from the more regular pattern in one way or another. The farms described in this chapter show three sorts of modifications: the first, that of a kinship tie between tenant and landlord; the second, various social pathologies; the third, management of a farm by a woman. These three by no means encompass the range of modifications, but they are suggestive of the sorts of deviations existing. The topical analysis in Part II, although focused on the activities of the mothers, also shows the range of variation in many matters which relate to the farming situation, such as neighborhoods, size of farms, houses, supplementary income, and credit sources.

Farm Nine: A Poor Relation

Of the modifications of landlord-tenant relations to a more personal plane, none is more common than that caused by the existence of family connections between them. The modification is so great in the case of a son "tending" his father's or father-in-law's land that the son can hardly be regarded as completely identified with the tenant group. On the other hand, the stability of many rural communities makes for a prevalence of kinship ties, with third and fourth cousins so common that they are granted very few special economic privileges, although their social prestige may be somewhat enhanced because "they came from good stock." Between these degrees of kinship we have chosen first cousinship to illustrate a middle ground.

A certain sharecropper is first cousin on his mother's side to his landlord, who is the leading citizen in a small village a mile away from the farm. Here the landlord owns and operates a thriving general merchandise store, where horse collars, singletrees, churns, bananas, Shirley Temple dolls, suspenders, and silk hose are all displayed in the front show window. In the back of the store a section is partitioned off and labeled with a "No Admittance" sign, where he presides as postmaster over thirty-five post boxes. He owns over a dozen farms in the neighborhood, most of them acquired gradually from profits of his store and therefore noncontiguous.

Yet the landlord is not entirely a self-made man, as one can tell from the appearance of his "home place" now occupied by his sharecropper cousin. The substantially built, two-story house, set on a hill crest under fine old shade trees, still looks respectable in spite of the rear view one gets of it through barns and outbuildings from the highway, which has been recently relocated. And although the sharecropper's wife complains of its poor repair—that the weatherboarding is rotting off, the roof leaking—the house is far better in original construction and upkeep than a nonrelated tenant might hope for. Living in this old family home with a graveyard of common ancestors on the place makes for social recognition and acceptance not granted to other sharecroppers living nearby.

The members of this family did not have to start from the bottom in general cultural advantages when they began sharecropping. The man had finished high school, taken a short business course in a city, and "clerked" in his cousin's store for fifteen years. He gave up this job when a lumber company opened up in the village and offered him a better paying job keeping time and hauling. Then an attack of typhoid fever kept him in bed for six months and left him without job or savings and with a family of nine to support. Although he does not like farming, he took the only occupational opportunity offered and became a sharecropper on his cousin's home place about ten years ago. With two mules supplied by his cousin and with the labor of his wife and children he has raised about eight acres of tobacco and a considerable portion of his food and feed each year. Some years have been better than others, but, after paying half of all his proceeds to the landlord, he has never had enough left over to buy a car or truck, or even to buy a team that he might raise his status to that of share tenant.

The family have definitely higher "standards" of living than are common in their economic class. Their furniture, acquired during the "clerking" period, is somewhat shabby but at least is sufficient to equip a living room which is neither a bedroom nor a kitchen. The mother when summoned from her room to see the visitor took time to change to a fresh cotton dress and to don her only pair of hose. The alert and attractive children showed excellent and cordial manners in greeting and entertaining a stranger until their mother appeared. And yet the consciousness of standards far higher than can be achieved on their very low income seems to intensify the sense of economic frustration. The same desires which make for positive motivation, for ambition, increase the awareness of deprivation in this situation, where there seems to be no path of escape open. Every fall when the crop is in the farmer swears he will never "tend" on halves again because the returns are not worth the labor that goes into it. Yet each spring, because he can find no other job, nothing else to do, he plants again in desperation.

A recent catastrophe aggravated their economic plight. Last summer shortly before harvesting time a severe hailstorm ruined all the best leaves of their tobacco. Since they had no insurance their year's labor was practically destroyed in one afternoon. Several members of the family set out to seek some supplementary income. The father left to his wife and younger children the salvaging of the remaining tobacco, its curing and grading, and went to Georgia to work in a tobacco warehouse. The oldest son went to a CCC camp, which meant $15 a month for the family. The oldest daughter, twenty, went to work in a cotton mill in the county. These extra jobs made things look brighter for a short period, but the father's warehouse work lasted only two months, the son had to leave the camp located in a swamp area because of chronic respiratory trouble, and the mill closed down at Christmas time for an indefinite period.

There is no money in the household now and none of the recent efforts of various members of the family has succeeded in securing any. The mother has applied for work in the WPA sewing room in a town ten miles away but has not been accepted. She feels that whatever help the government *can* extend to families should be given to the mothers since they have had long experience in stretching pennies and managing. She believes that with ten or fifteen dollars a month she could meet the family's urgent needs even with the expenses of four children in school, commencement approaching, and a fourteen-year-old son in bed for a year with inflammatory rheumatism. The only chance she can see for getting even a few cents a week is for herself and her daughter laid off from the cotton mill to start stringing tobacco sacks. Because of the extra labor available, the result of the mill layoffs, the price has been reduced to forty cents a thousand—for clipping, turning, stringing, knotting, and tying in bunches of twenty-five the small sacks in which smoking tobacco is sold for a nickel. This means that an adult can hardly make more than ten cents a day at it, for time and money are consumed in getting them and carrying them back to town. It is an unpleasant and unprofitable last resort, but it is the only employment to be had at the present. (This sweatshop industry was abolished in North Carolina in the fall of 1938 when the Wages and Hours Bill went into effect.)

Because there is no other way out, they are going to work on halves again this year. Their planting is not delayed by waiting for acreage and market allotments to be announced, because their landlord will be given an allotment for all his farms together and, since he is a cousin, he will not cut them down below what they want to raise. This matter is typical of the sort of privilege a poor relation may expect from his landlord kinsman. The favors shown are in such things as house assignment or market allotment whereby not the landlord but other tenants suffer. There are no adjustments of rental shares or division of the fertilizer bill, where favoring would have to come out of the owner's pocket.

Farm Ten: Pathological Sharecropping

The two modal practices of share rentals are the payment of one-fourth of the cotton or tobacco and one-third of the corn and other grain by the share tenant owning his stock and implements, and the payment of one-half of everything by the sharecropper contributing only the labor of himself and his family. There are modifications and local adaptations of these practices as there are of the common rule of paying the same fraction of the seed and fertilizer bill that each will get of the crop. In one county, where the land is quite rich, it is customary for the share tenant to pay one-third of the money crop as well as of the grain. In another county quite a few share tenants who furnish their own teams pay half to the landlord, who in these cases furnishes all the fertilizer and seed. A more unusual deviation from the general arrangements is found on a cotton farm in the southern part of the area we have been describing.

The sharecropper on this farm is in a bad bargaining position. A minimum of household furnishings is his only possession; his livestock consists of one 'possum caught by his children and being fattened for Thanksgiving dinner. His labor force is below par in both quantity and quality. His own health is impaired by diabetes, "high blood," and rheumatism, which has drawn one of his legs up much shorter than the other. His second wife, whose two children are in an institution for the feeble-minded, is of low mentality herself and rather frail although a steady field worker. Since his oldest son ran away from home last year, his seventeen-year-old daughter has had to do most of the plowing because he himself is too crippled to plow. A fifteen-year-old boy is an epileptic and can do nothing except very simple manual tasks in the house. The twin sister of this boy is extremely undersized but works regularly in the field when she is not in school, as does a still younger girl of thirteen. Because of these handicaps the sharecropper has not been able to "come out even" in many years and he can no longer get credit from landlords, loan agencies, or merchants.

The absentee owner also has certain deficiencies to be met. He was brought up on an adjacent farm, where his brother now lives, but has moved to town and no longer has a team since his only other holding is worked by his nephew as a share tenant. Therefore, the following arrangement has been worked out. The sharecropper works one day a week for the landlord's brother in exchange for the use of his team for plowing. But because it is the landlord's duty to supply the team, he pays the sharecropper for this work one dollar a week. This weekly dollar has to cover all the family's living expenses since the landlord will not furnish any cash or "stand" for the sharecropper's accounts at stores. The sharecropper can not get credit of any kind and so the landlord supplies all the seed and fertilizer. Because of this the fraction the landlord gets of the crop is increased from the customary one-half to two-thirds. He gets two-thirds of not only the cotton but also everything raised, including "patches" of such produce as peas, which must all be shelled by the epileptic boy before they are divided.

This family have had troubles this year other than economic and health. A three-pound baby was born to the unmarried, seventeen-year-old daughter right in the midst of the cotton picking season. She "blames" it on a boy from another neighborhood where they used to live, but the welfare officials are inclined to believe that there has been incest. It is rumored that the father ran his oldest son off from home last year when the boy tried to stop the father's relations with the daughter.

The seventeen-year-old mother looks younger than she is with her round, childish, freckled face and a sunny smile. She alone of her family registered normal on the intelligence tests administered by the officials who were considering sterilization after the birth of her baby. In the field she is her father's "right hand man" and at home she manages the household and takes the hostess' responsibility in entertaining visitors while her timid stepmother retires to the kitchen. As the baby lost weight on her breast milk for the first six weeks, the clinic advised that she change to a bottle. Without a cow, ice, money for buying milk, or training in preparing it, she has found this very difficult. For one week's supply the "Welfare" gave her a can of powdered milk but she fixed too much at once and it soured and made the baby sick. She was hoping her aunt's cow would freshen soon and she could send her little sister two miles every day to get milk, but the aunt has decided to move away. In spite of these difficulties the baby has survived and regardless of parentage is the pet and pride of the family. The children take turns walking or rocking her if she cries even the tiniest bit at night.

The family have very few visits and very little aid from neighbors. One reason is that they have moved so often they have no friends of long standing. They wanted to move again this year because they felt that two-thirds was too much to pay to a landlord. Their own share of the four bales of cotton they made this year was not enough to buy a pair of shoes around. But the father could not find any other place to go; moreover, he thought it might be a good idea to stay on one place for two years so that he could plant wheat in the fall in order that they might have at least flour next year. They have also raised sweet potatoes, cane for syrup, and field peas to supply them adequately for a year. These were displayed rather proudly by the children in the one of their four rooms which serves as a storehouse.

The Welfare Department has helped the family with clothes for the two children in school and with a few other incidentals. The Department supplied the mosquito netting through which one could hardly see the baby for the moving layer of flies on the outside. They have furnished medical treatment for several members of the family and medicine for the epileptic boy, which "keeps him down to about two fits a week." It is doubtful, however, if adequate social case work could achieve satisfactory rehabilitation of this family.

The combination of economic, health, and mental liabilities has produced a social pathology here. While such an extreme case is by no means typical, it does illustrate in exaggerated form conditions prevelant in many tenant families above the border line of destitution.

Farm Eleven: A Mother Manages

In every region of the United States the percentage of women who are widowed or divorced is considerably lower in rural farm than in nonfarm areas. A farm woman bereft of her husband often remarries quickly, moves into town or village, or is absorbed into some relative's family. Tradition prescribes that a farm needs a man both for the heavy, manual work, such as chopping wood and plowing, and for the managerial and financial ability required. Yet here and there a woman takes over the running of a farm, usually from necessity. One such mother is to be described here although on several counts she cannot be called typical. She is divorced rather than widowed. She began farming alone when her oldest son was only twelve and has retained the managing position. Although only a sharecropper, she has been successful enough during her ten years of farming without benefit of a husband that she has been in need of relief only once for a short period, and last year she came out far enough ahead to buy a second-hand automobile.

A résumé of her life illustrates several other points of atypicality. She was not born or brought up on a farm, as is the rule, but in a mill village. She went to work in a cotton mill at the age of eleven after a minimum of schooling and worked there for sixteen years until her first son was born. Her first marriage at twenty-five was late, and even more unusual was the Enoch Arden behavior of her husband, a World War soldier reported dead, who reappeared after her second marriage. She chose to keep the second husband because he "*would* work sometimes," and they began farming twenty years ago. As his health failed she did a larger and larger part of the field work while he stayed home to look after the baby. Finally when his drinking became almost continuous, the friction between them unbearable, and his health quite bad, she divorced him, and he went to a government sanitarium.

This happened ten years ago. Her children were all under twelve years of age and she could not find a landlord who would take her with five small children and no man. A kind old man in the spirit of neighborliness and "helping widows and orphans" finally let her move to an unused house on his land. Early in the spring some tenants moved away unexpectedly and she prevailed upon him to let her take over their tobacco crop. Her twelve-year-old boy did the plowing and her nine-year-old boy learned how the next year. The mother did almost everything else, even to staying up at nights to take care of the fire in the curing barns. She says she "never had no noon"; while the others were eating or sitting around she had all the housework to do. Things like sewing, mending, and canning had to be done at night. Neighbors volunteer testimonials to her industry—"she ain't got a lazy bone in her body."

With her children practically "raised"—the youngest is twelve now—she can take things a little easier. It is well she can because her health is "giving out" after all that work, her blood pressure is about one hundred and seventy and her eyes are failing. But it is only the hardest work which she forswears. She still does most of the grading of the tobacco and all of the managing of the farm. She would have bought a mule when they came out ahead last fall but the landlord wants to work his own team on this place. She doesn't want to move since this seems like home after ten years of living here even though the house is just a three-room log cabin. One of her sons who has a job in a grocery store in town started buying a second-hand Model A Ford but could not keep up the payments. So she bought out his interest, paid the balance owed, and now speaks proudly of "my car."

This woman of forty-nine is a strange mixture of ancient and modern, conservative and progressive. Most unusual is her keen interest in politics and in other national and world affairs. She has decided views about such matters and expresses them without hesitation or timidity. She deplores the present depression, thinks it will get worse as election time approaches because that always makes for more insecurity, but believes that neither Republicans nor Democrats can do anything about the depression because it is caused by machines displacing men from jobs and there not being enough work to go around. She illustrates her points with concrete examples from her observations in both farming and the textile industry. She listens tolerantly to minor protests from her grown son, but considers her judgment far superior to his on such matters—an unusual attitude for a tenant farm mother. She is equally sure about crop control's being for the best. Her regret is that so many people are already sick of it—even some of those who voted for it but received small allotments—and she is afraid they will not vote for it next year. She thinks they should consider in terms of two or three years the cumulative effect of control or no control, but she knows most of them are short-sighted and think only of what they can get at the minute.

She will suffer badly from being cut this year, but she is just as glad not to be able to have such a big crop since she should not work quite so hard now. She has had as many as seven acres but she thinks they will be allowed only five this year. The landlord has not yet apportioned his allotted eleven acres among his three tenants, but, since he is now too old to farm himself, it ought to be divided out fairly. The landlord has always been good to her and she and her children, in turn, work for him on his garden patches without being paid for it.

Tobacco and corn are the main crops grown. The land is not good for wheat and, although they have a garden and do some canning, the beetle has become so bad that she can no longer count on getting enough canned to last through the winter. They killed one hog this year, but of course that will not supply meat throughout the year. All the children except one seem to have survived the diet without serious injury to health. The exception is the nineteen-year-old boy who works in town. He has had rickets and has never been strong enough to do regularly the hard physical work involved in farming.

In this mother's attitudes and practices, the past is visible in her response to the paternalism of her landlord and in her ideas about "whipping children plenty and starting them to work early to bring them up right." The present is evident in her emphasis on the cash crop to the exclusion of food needs. The future is suggested in her growing interest in "what the world is coming to" and "why" and in her political articulateness. She neither complains unduly over her past hardships nor worries too much about the future, yet she shows a larger comprehension of both past and future in her interpretation of the present than does the modal tenant mother. Whether she has been able to accomplish what she has done because she had advanced ideas, or whether her ideas have been advanced through her life and experience in areas commonly reserved for men, she exemplifies a stage in both ideas and achievement beyond that reached by most of her sisters.

Part II · Mothers

Chapter 6

Of Tenant Women

"At home with the farm tenant mother" might well be the verdict on even first visits to these women. "I ain't so busy I can't stop to talk awhile, so come right in!" Such was the sincere welcome which came from many a woman interrupted while washing up the dinner dishes or doing other household tasks, as expressing her liking for company and talk in spite of the never ending round of waiting duties.

"The colored woman you saw leaving is an old 'granny' who stays with women when—when they're sick, you know. She was telling me that Martha Dean's new baby. . . ." An account of current neighborhood happenings began the conversation in the combination kitchen-dining-living room. Then talk went on to many subjects—to farm and crops, to children and school, to health and pregnancies, to hopes and troubles. Children arrived on the school bus, ate sweet potatoes saved from dinner, and changed into old clothes for evening chores. The husband passed through the room and lingered for a few minutes to discuss the weather and crop control. Afternoon wore on and the pleasant stay ended with kindly protestations—"You don't have to hurry off so soon."

In several ways this visit was typical of first meetings with the mothers: in their cordial reception of a stranger, indicative of their welcome to a break in routine and isolation; in their explanation of the immediate situation in which they are engaged as a technique of hospitality and of supplying leads for conversation; in their readiness to talk of their children, homes, work, and even more intimate matters if certain conventions are observed in approach and phraseology; and in the opportunity afforded to observe directly their family relations and some of the day's work. Second and subsequent visits often led to increased confidence and to more intimate revelations. The locations varied with season and weather. Kitchens, bedrooms, porches, tobacco striphouses, and cotton fields served as settings for the informal interviews. Some mothers kept on with the work at hand and some seized the excuse to rest and courteously gave their full attention to the talk and visit. There were all sorts of situations. Some visits were strictly private and uninterrupted; during others children came in and out, babies were nursed, neighbors dropped in, or the whole family was together working in the striphouse.

The tenant women varied widely in general appearance. It seems appropriate to give brief, sample descriptions to suggest the heterogeneity of the group before summarizing details of dress, health, speech, and education.

Mrs. Perry is of medium height but quite hunched for her forty years. She is slim except for her protruding abdomen which is no doubt due to her having borne sixteen children since her marriage at fifteen. The pattern of her dingy, faded cotton dress, her black, ribbed, lisle hose, and high-topped shoes suggest old-fashionedness, yet she speaks her mind directly with little circumlocution and no timidity. She has no time for primping, and stringy bits of colorless hair show beneath a "stocking" cap on her head. She has no make-up on her face—only brownish snuff stains at the corners of her mouth.

Next, a plump and pretty widow of thirty daintily arrayed in a clean, gingham dress with a ruffled organdie apron. Her black, bobbed hair is naturally wavy and attractively arranged. Her face dimples and her eyes sparkle as she tells of what high prices she gets for her tobacco when she takes it to market herself. She boasts of her strength in doing farm work and also of her shrewdness in managing. She doesn't want to marry again—she explains with a twinkle that she doesn't have to because all the men in the neighborhood help her whenever she needs it.

Frailty and a childish expression make tiny Mrs. Travis look younger than her twenty-eight years. A tattered dress is her only garment and she draws her bare feet underneath her as she crouches timidly on an unmade bed. She explains that she doesn't mind telling things if there's no writing but she is suspicious of "sign-ups" because she has no "learning." Her cough breaks into each sentence but she doesn't know whether she has tuberculosis or not because she hasn't had money enough to go to a doctor in five years.

The mother who manages Farm Eleven presents an air of respectability with gold rimmed glasses, carefully mended rayon hose, and a neat black and white checkered dress. Adorning her bosom is her most treasured possession—a gold plated brooch containing miniatures of herself and a girl friend taken when they were eighteen. Her graying hair is combed back straight, but neatly, to a knot now stylishly high. Her features and manner suggest her strength of will and pride in accomplishment.

A sturdy, almost stocky, blond mother with squarish features is quite composed and placid. She manages her three young children easily with no trace of annoyance at their interruptions. She answers questions smilingly, but shows little imagination in conversation. Her neat, gingham dress, anklets, and tennis slippers of the first visit are replaced by a faded jumper and bare feet on another day when she has been scrubbing all the floors of her house, but her unruffled manner remains the same.

"I'm splitting out of my clothes like a grasshopper," said one mother as she tried to hold together the most exposing holes on the day before her last child was born. This was literally true and she has not had on a pair of shoes since her feet began to swell at the beginning of pregnancy. Yet with uncombed hair and unwashed face she joked with all present and kept up a running stream of anecdotes about how landlords cheat tenants and about how much "meanness" children learn at school nowadays. Unabashed, she sent a child to the mantel for a comb and then worked on her own and the child's matted hair during the conversation. The work was intermittent, for she would stop to gesticulate with the comb or to slap one of her many children with it.

An Old Age Assistance recipient wears an old-fashioned calico dress which comes to her ankles and a matched, wide-brimmed bonnet.

She has coughed ever since she had measles forty years ago and leaning over to ease the pain in her chest has made her very hunched. Her face is deeply lined, her hands are swollen with rheumatism, and yet she still does field work for a half day at a time. She manages her slight weight in a surprisingly agile fashion for her age as she jumps over the broken steps of the porch to get to her flowers where she stops to comment on the beauty of individual blossoms while she picks a "bouquet" for the visitor.

Mrs. Chapman came from the potato patch with an air of embarrassment. She explained her bulging appearance was due to having on two dresses—an old one on top to protect the better one underneath. She kept her hand over her mouth until she felt enough at ease to explain that her plates had always hurt so much that she wore them only to church or when she knew company was coming. Then she quickly forgot her appearance and her eyes gleamed with sincerity as she launched into a theological discussion expressing her views on "close communion."

A care-free, overalled, barefoot, twenty-two-year-old mother, egged on by the teasing of her mother and sister, boasted of many things—of how her husband never went in debt even for fertilizer, of how long they had lived in one place, of how large and healthy her children were, of how little trouble it had been to bear four children in seven years, of how she started using snuff when she was ten. Her face was tanned, her hair sunbleached, and her body raw-boned. She walked with the combination of exaggerated stride and suggestion of slouch which is typical of farming men.

A mother up too early from bearing her thirteenth child was lying in bed clad in a heavy outing gown. Not yet forty, her hair was iron gray. Her features, like her body, were long and gaunt. There was despair and hopelessness in her countenance. She smiled only when petting her baby. When she got up to mend the fire she explained that she wore shoes and stockings to bed since she must get up often to "tend" the four youngest children while the older ones are in school.

With all these differences existing, it is yet possible to indicate the modal pattern and the range of variation in many specific details. Over half of the women were between thirty-five and forty-five years of age although every five-year age group was represented, from a young, unmarried mother of seventeen to a still vigorous one of "somp'n over seventy, I ain't sure." In health there was none permanently bed-ridden and yet only one who had absolutely no complaints. "High blood," "low blood," bad teeth, piles, lacerations, pellagra (six active cases), pregnancy, varicose veins, anaemia, rheumatism, a "nervous heart"—they ran the whole gamut of common folks' troubles. Perhaps because there was a selection of mothers with large families, female troubles were most commonly reported, and because of age distribution, complaints of "the change working on me" were frequent.

In dress there was a prevailing mode: a cotton dress, faded but otherwise in fairly good condition, a well-worn and usually ragged sweater in cool weather, no hose, shoes out at the toes and run over at the heels. None was seen barefoot in winter although many of them wore no shoes in summer. Variations from the mode were numerous but not without limits. No one of them wore a more elaborate dress than a ruffled cotton house frock, none had on French heels, very few used make-up or finger nail polish, and the half dozen who had permanents had not been to beauty parlors to have them set into waves recently enough for the effects to be discernible. The best dressed woman wore a spick-and-span dark blue broadcloth dress with a prim starched collar, an embroidered apron, silk hose, and two-tone, saddle sport shoes. In the other direction, many had ragged and torn dresses; several wore overalls. In summer it was evident that a few had on no underwear, but in winter none was without some sort of wrap for warmth, even if it were only an old, discarded man's coat.

In their speech certain colloquialisms and errors in grammar were almost universal: double and sometimes triple negatives, "done" and "seen" as past tense, "ain't" and "ary," occasionally "haint" and "nary," "like" as a conjunction, "don't" with the third person singular. Only one mother, however, made the sort of errors attributable to a conscious striving toward better English—"between he and the church," "like I and my husband"—and deliberately used the correct "rear" in answer to a question about "raising" children.

Idioms and unusual word usages enliven their conversation. For example, the next-to-the-youngest child is always the "knee-baby," no matter how old he gets to be. "Evening" is afternoon, differentiated from "night," which means from supper onward. An admired landlord is the "stoutest" man in the community, the menopause is "when nature leaves you," midwives are "grannies," helped takes its older form "holp," a baby is "smart" if it doesn't cry, and a child is "shrewd" who makes good marks at school. Forthright expressions are "so hungry I could eat up a storm," "our preacher's got a lot of mess to him." Some words or phrases imply modesty or good manners. One example is the prefacing of every opinion or generalization with, "It seems like . . ." while slightly less self-effacing variants are, "I allus say . . ." or "I tells 'em. . . ." Some begin every response with an almost servile "Yep'm . . ." or "Yap'm. . . ." "Kind of" with its variants, "kinder" and the more gentle "kindly," vie with "right smart" as favorite specifications of degree.

Since ninety percent of these women were born in the State in which they live—nearly half of them in the same county where they are living now—and over ninety percent of them were brought up on farms, their schooling has been mainly of the preconsolidation rural type. Two of the three who had finished high school had one additional year of education, one in a teachers' college and one in a junior college. In contrast, eighteen of the women—or about one in seven—were illiterate, while the mean educational level achieved was five grades.

Imagination and ability to talk did not seem to be closely

correlated with number of grades completed. The old lady over seventy who never got out of the first grade—she went to school only a few days each year because her mother kept her bright children out to work and let the ones who learned more slowly have more chances at schooling—was by far the best humorist of them all. She grasped quickly what sort of things interested the visitor, selected pertinent incidents, told them with exaggerations for entertainment, and all the while was highly amused herself. Another one who had "stopped out in the fourth" displayed a mastery of vivid and graphic detail in her conversation. Still another who had never gone to high school had at her tongue's end the most inexhaustible store of anecdotes of actual happenings to illustrate any feature of country life or even any moral or generalization one might suggest. At the other end of the scale there was one too feeble-minded to answer much more than "Yes'm" or "No'm," and in several instances lack of imagination was a drawback where there was evident willingness to answer questions asked but very little of the spontaneous offerings most desired.

The horizons of these mothers are not appreciably enlarged by assimilation of what has been stored in the printed page. The modal practice with regard to reading is, "Not much—I don't have time." Of those who can read, the lower extreme is, "Nothing—I don't care nothing about it—I don't even read the Bible." Only one mother had a sizable collection of books, which included, in addition to novels, semiscientific treatises on child psychology. This mother had attended during the past year several "literary" lectures at a nearby university and was the only mother visited who had ever utilized any of the services other than hospital offered by the several centers of higher education in the area. A more typical response of those who do read is the following:

"I read whatever I can get aholt of. We don't take no

magazines or papers but my daughter comes home from the mill every week-end and allus brings me magazines—*True Story* and things like that. It don't make much difference what I'm reading so long as it passes the time and gets my mind off'n work. John allus wants to go to bed right after supper, so I set up and read. When you work all day and just set in the night thinking about all there is *to* do, reading is the best thing to get your mind off'n it."

Scant reading material is available. Children's school books, the Bible, and farmers' magazines are most frequent, with a few daily papers, a scattering of farm home or housekeeping magazines, and in two homes urban women's magazines such as *McCall's* and *The Ladies' Home Journal*. The modal comment on farm papers is, "I look at the poultry and garden sections sometimes." One enthusiastic reader, however, hopes they will never have to be without their *Progressive Farmer* again as they were in the depression. None of the women has ever used travelling libraries although these services are offered in several of the counties. When one couple was told about such libraries the husband expressed the hope that it would never start coming down their road because he knew he'd never get his supper cooked on time if his wife had new things to read every two weeks. Where there are grown daughters at home *pulps* are more frequent, and of all periodicals called by name *True Story* was most often mentioned.

In the four-fifths of the homes without radios specific interest or concrete information on current affairs is rare. The question most often asked by the mothers, excluding crop prices and policies—was "What about these foreign wars?" But only some of those with radios and one other mother who read regularly her daughter's high school current events weekly had more than the vaguest knowledge about international affairs. Two illustrations of extreme ignorance follow. One mother said, "There's a right smart talk now about the fighting. I sho' do hope this State (North Carolina) don't go into it." When another woman working in the striphouse deplored "Germany being so mean," her husband agreed, "Yes, we ought to have killed him in the last war." This led to a prolonged debate as to whether the Kaiser and Hitler were the same person. Usually the reaction to the eventuality of war was in terms of sons, husbands, or brothers of military age, although there were occasional nationalistic sentiments expressed. One mother thought the United States should give Japan a lesson after the *Panay* incident and another that we would finally have to go "straighten Europe out again."

The limited range of interest is partly explainable by the fact that three-fourths of them had spent their entire lives on farms with no other occupation than housekeeping, bearing and rearing children, and farming. Four-fifths of those who had worked at other things had been in cotton or hosiery mills. Preference between farm and mill work varied with age. All of the older ex-cotton mill workers were for the farm and country and listed grievances against mills and mill towns. Two of them had been put into the mills before they were ten years old and thus got no education. Two of them claimed that the mills had ruined their health. Almost all of them felt that mill towns were very bad places for bringing up children. Several of the younger ones, however, preferred mill work because of the cash money it brings in. One of these showed a bedroom suite she had bought while doing factory work and another boasted of what fine clothes she had been able to afford then. Other occupations reported were tobacco and box factory workers, telephone operator, teacher, and domestic servant, but none of these was represented by more than two mothers.

In order that specific interests would be revealed, the direction of conversation was left to the mother as far as possible after important topics such as children, work, health, and neighborhoods had been discussed. This was done even more on second and following visits after a fair degree of rapport had been established. The most common response to a freedom of selection of subject matter was an introduction of some "problem"—an account of at least the external factors involved in some situation over which the mother worried. These "problems," as may be expected, never transcended the bounds of their daily lives either geographically or intellectually. Their roots and implications in the larger social world were rarely given more recognition or thought than a vague generalization. "I suppose all children are harder to control nowadays," "Young people don't behave the way they used to," "I guess no farmer makes any money now," or "I guess there just ain't enough jobs to go around." The majority of the problems related to economic matters or to family affairs, frequently to aspects of bringing up children. Their content is described in later chapters dealing with these subjects.

Attitudes toward the interviewer are so important in conditioning the content and coloring of information given that their manifestations should be described. As has been stated, there was in every case an initial cordiality which made visiting possible. This was due largely to the prevailing pattern of hospitality if there is no suspicion or prejudice aroused rather than to any immediate positive reaction to the visitor. Attitudes developed later are best shown in the uses the mothers made of the relationship with the visitor. Several mothers definitely tried to get relief or financial aid of some sort, although this gradually became less dominant as they realized the visitor had no official connections with the welfare or farm security agencies. One widow did not tell at first of all her eleven children who might be helping support her and dwelt at length on her hard luck in being left with a crippled child and without support. She took the rôle of "rich lady's poor" and told story after story, all leading to the moral of unselfishness and the beauty of sharing with others. On later visits, probably convinced of the futility of her efforts by lack of results, she responded more nearly according to the modal pattern to be described. Another seemed never to give up the hope that the visitor could do something about getting her husband's veterans' pension restored and her conversation constantly recurred to their need for this. Yet this was by no means her only use of the visitor, for her friendliness did not abate and she always said good-bye with, "Come again, because you know I *do* like to talk."

In contrast several mothers accepted the visitor as approximately an equal. One sought identification for social recognition. She insisted the visit be prolonged one afternoon until her pastor came. In conversation she constantly emphasized that country women with cars could now be just like town women, they could go to town to club meetings, to movies, etc. Another, without condescending, was most anxious to oblige since her home demonstration agent had requested it. Her husband would not relinquish the notion that here was a government agent sent to find out just how country people lived. The two of them patiently and graciously explained how they got along so well by crop rotation, home production of food and feed, and by not devoting all their time to a cash crop. They were justifiably proud of their economic position and expressed the wish that Roosevelt himself could come and see how well farm families can live if they all work hard and raise their food so that they can spend their tobacco money for other things. This use of the visitor as an ambassador to the President probably gave their accounts a rosy and optimistic hue.

The modal use of the visitor, however, was simply as a

person to talk to—evidently superior in education and economic status, but not too far removed from former country ways of living to be able to understand. There was often some puzzling at first over why anyone who wasn't an "agent" wanted to visit, but the direct answer of interest in women who lived in the country seemed satisfactory to most. To specific questions about vocation the answer of part-time teaching was given since the concept of research was outside the realm of their experience content. In a few cases where there was an intelligent interest the research project was partly explained but it was very difficult to get the idea across. Even the former teacher, who was delighted to cooperate, could conceive of the project only as getting material for one of those government "statistic" reports. It occurred to only one bright high school daughter to ask, "Are you writing a book?" To this and other questions frank and honest replies were given and there was no deception of any sort even though there could not be complete explanation. The mothers seemed to respond more to the sympathetic interest of a person who enjoyed listening to whatever they wished to talk about rather than to any exact rôle or status of the interviewer. There was often noticeable transfer with increase in confidences given. Emotional release was observable in certain individuals, although the grosser manifestations of this accompanied accounts of bereavements rather than of inner conflicts.

The pattern of courtesy and manners exhibited most frequently included giving the visitor the best chair, inviting her to take off her hat and coat, apologizing for dirty clothes or house, or for spitting—about half of them used snuff—conventionally protesting her leaving, and inviting her to come back —"Now don't let this be your last visit." Extra courtesies were frequent: several excused themselves with phrases which would grace a drawing room when there were necessary interruptions, others sent children to draw fresh water from the well on hot days or to close car windows when it rained. Two instances of car trouble brought ready help. There were all sorts of gifts of produce—watermelons, cantaloupes, quinces, pumpkins, apples, raspberries, jars of preserves and jellies, liver pudding, cake, flowers, and popcorn—many of them presented on first visits. A number of invitations to meals and cornshuckings, to a family reunion and a church meeting were extended as well as several to "come spend the day." A common technique of entertaining was to show all the snapshots and photographs of various members of the family and to relate incidents suggested by the pictures. On the other hand, there were those who were unacquainted with the niceties of good manners. Some of these did not get up when the visitor arrived or left and spat without excuses. One hiccoughed and belched frequently without even interrupting her conversation. Several accosted in the yard or on the porch did not invite the visitor in to sit down although they voluntarily discussed many of the most intimate details of life in an hour's visit with both standing.

Personality characteristics do not lend themselves to generalizations easily. The more concrete aspects of life are categorized in later chapters, but the less tangible, less enumerable qualities are evasive and elusive of summary descriptions. Here we merely suggest some common personality traits inferred from the concrete manifestations illustrated later.

Quite impressive is the utilitarian and basic emphasis derived from an "all work" program. Frills and furbelows, imagination and introspection, superficial and artificial pursuits have little time or place in the thinking and acting of these women. Of more importance, however, is the emotional maturity evidenced in their acceptance of economic hardship. Such acceptance can not be termed passive for it involves a constant output of labor that even a subsistence living may be obtained. It is mature in the sense that activities are directed toward the objective factors of the situation—toward farm, children, home—rather than toward inner goals demanded by inferiority feelings or other internal maladjustments. It is, however, unintelligent in the sense of not being based upon a careful consideration of the factors underlying the primary obstacles and a subsequent planning of a less laborious means of accomplishing the business of living. Nowhere, however, is there a more complete example of the environmental explanation of such unintelligent action. Economic necessity leaves no time for intellectual contemplation of the problem; educational training has supplied neither content nor tools for its solution; isolation has prevented the stimulation from contact with people and diffusion of more efficient techniques; the culturally inherited ideology holds the mothers to their tasks and in their places with the sanction of God and the Southern tradition; and the "system" provides no escape.

Chapter 7

Of Field Work

ONE MIGHT imagine that these mothers of large families would be so occupied with childbearing and caring, with cooking, washing, sewing, and cleaning, that they would of necessity have their activities circumscribed by the four walls of home—or at most by the boundaries of yard, garden, and outhouse. This is not at all true. While the women yield to their husbands the prerogative of planning and managing the farm, of assigning tasks and directing the family's labor on it, of selling the crop at their own discretion and pocketing the proceeds, they nevertheless have an active interest in the farms and crops often exceeding that in the home. Their knowledge of farming matters is surprising and pertains not only to the immediate condition of the current crop but to details of renting, credit, the sequence of operations, and to the basic data for making an estimate of how they will "come out this year."

So universal is this interest in farming that the topic offered a handy escape in interviewing impasses. Recourse to "crops" as a subject on which the mother felt safe and at home alleviated timidity in the early stages and embarrassment after very intimate revelations in the later. The mother of a feeble-minded child was at first unwilling to talk of her children but warmed cordially on the subject of tobacco as she proudly told of being the only one in the family who could grade it right. On later visits the greeting, "How are you getting along?" sometimes brought forth a history of health since the last visit but more often a review of specific and general farm conditions: that they turned out one hundred and twenty-five barrels of corn at their shucking last week, that cotton prices had dropped so low and theirs was so scattered it was hardly worth picking over again, that the hail had ruined the best leaves of their tobacco, or that tobacco was bringing better prices now than they had hoped for.

The sort of farm information offered by different mothers may be illustrated by the following typical bits: that the rain had drowned out six and a half of their ten acres of tobacco; that they had got thirty-five hundred pounds from a small cotton patch the first time over; that they had planted forty thousand hills of tobacco, five thousand hills to the acre—although this mother could not do the necessary division to calculate the number of acres; a lucid and detailed description of each process in producing a tobacco crop up to the marketing stage—she had never been to a sale; an account of the ravages of the boll weevil, which would cut the yield from five acres of cotton to half a bale; a listing of all the different renting arrangements in the neighborhood according to the fractions of each crop paid and the variations in supplying fertilizer and team; an exposition of a complicated system of cane syrup division whereby the man who owns the syrup mill gets the first three gallons for "setting down," then of every five in addition he gets one, the landowner one, and the tenants three.

There were a few women who professed no interest in or knowledge about such matters. One woman, desirous of identifying herself with the "town" women of a small village four miles away, insisted that she knew nothing of what went on outside of the house, which was her domain, that she had no idea of how her husband ran his business (farm), that she would be utterly helpless about farming if her husband should die, and that she felt women should devote all their time to homemaking. She gave herself away a little later when another visitor arrived by saying that he would have caught her in the striphouse if the men hadn't been measuring up corn today, by reporting that her husband had gotten $100 more than he expected from his tobacco last week, and finally by bragging on her daughter for having done all the cooking for the family last fall while she herself worked at getting the crop in the barn.

A second avowal of ignorance was more sincere, the result of an urban background in another State where the woman had been a telephone operator. She knew little and cared less for her husband's farming, which seemed only to get them deeper into debt each year. She was anxious for him to change to driving a truck for a soft drink company, especially since a storage barn and their entire tobacco crop had burned up the day before with only enough insurance to pay their government loan for fertilizer. She devoutly wished never to see a farm again. An intermediate stage between complete ignorance and the usual familiarity was less specific knowledge qualified with, "You'll have to ask John if you want to know exactly," or a polite reference to him for answer if he were present.

The most completely farm-centered interests were manifested by a hunched but hale woman of sixty with a wrinkled and weathered face, only two teeth and those snuff covered, but with clear blue eyes which twinkled as she shrewdly surmized as to how "these here foreign wars" make cotton go down because they can't ship it, or confided her suspicions that "the government just don't know what *to* do to help the farmers even though they mean well." Her concern over the death of her husband's father in another part of the State was great because it meant loss of the husband's working time for nearly a week in the busiest season. It had kept them from getting the fodder off the cane and the leaves had carried the frost right down to the heart of the stalk and ruined it. This woman was quite willing to give information about her children and her home, but the intensity of her interest in the farm never let her stay away from that subject for long. The esteem in which she held the visitor fell when she was unable to give the latest cotton quotation after admitting she had seen a morning paper.

The widespread interest and knowledge in farming and the policy of letting the inclinations of the mothers govern the proportion of time spent on various subjects resulted in more factual and attitudinal information about their farms and crops than had been anticipated in a study not primarily concerned with the strictly agricultural or economic aspects of the lives of the tenant mothers. This information was at times supplemented by husbands or children present, but the substance of the following descriptions of their farms came from the mothers themselves.

Cotton was the cash crop on about one-fifth of the farms, tobacco on nearly three-fourths, and truck and miscellaneous on the remaining ones. One who raises cotton declared laughingly that "money" crop was no longer the right name for it. In the matter of cotton versus tobacco, all the women save one expressed a preference for the one which she herself was raising. To the cotton farm women tobacco is dirty, works the women to death, and means too much of a strain even if it does bring in more money. To the tobacco farm women, cotton growing is back-breaking work, fit only for "niggers," and doesn't pay enough to live on. Almost invariably the preference was explained, bolstered, or rationalized by a phrase which justifies any preference, "We're used to it," or "We was brought up to do it." The exception mentioned was one who had only recently changed to tobacco and didn't like it because it was not what she was used to. The number of acres planted in tobacco varied from one (the amount allotted to a new grower), through the modal interval of from three to five, to several cases of eleven acres, where the family was large or where some hired help was used. The amount in cotton ranged from subsidiary patches of one acre to several of fifteen. The greatest number of farms were two-horse, nearly as many were one-horse, and a few of combined families or of those with subtenants were three-horse.

Although cotton and tobacco were almost universally the primary cash crop, an excess over food and feed needs of corn, sweet potatoes, peas, cane syrup, wheat, or garden produce occasionally permitted some cash returns. The same situation obtained for livestock—the sale of an extra calf or hog was sometimes reported although these were likewise raised primarily for home use. The range of success in supplying home food needs was wide and not closely correlated with economic status. A fortunate family exulted in their ability to produce *all* they ate except coffee, sugar, salt, and a few fancy things, while another equally prosperous one buys much "store" food because they prefer it. A very hard up family have this fall for the first time in years the prospect of enough hog meat to last them through the winter, while a relief family produce almost all of their food.

The range of tenure classifications extends from a few who pay standing rent, cash or produce, to the sharecropper who pays two-thirds of everything he raises, with all sorts of intermediate rental practices. In general the share tenant who owns his stock and pays one-fourth of his cotton or tobacco and one-third of his grain is better off than the cropper who gets only one-half of what he produces for his labor. In the group visited there were about one and one-half times as many share tenants as sharecroppers. There are some inversions of the usual negative relationship between rental fractions and economic level, however. The most prosperous-appearing family visited pays one-half to their landlord, while a destitute family pays nothing to an owner who supplies them a house and land for patches since the old man at seventy-three is too feeble to "tend land" any longer, and all they produce is just what the children raise by "scratching."

There were deviations from the set classification of share tenant or sharecropper which affected the income of these families. Most common was some source of income, in addition to that from farming, earned by the husband from WPA or by working in a filling station on Saturdays, or running a grain mill during the winter, going to Canada to cure tobacco after his own crop was housed, hauling tobacco to market, driving a meat truck, doing farm work for a neighbor, or hunting or trapping in winter. In such cases farming was the man's chief occupation and the other jobs were supplementary. Two border-line cases were where husbands had full-time jobs at a tobacco factory in town and at a grist mill, while the mother and children had to do all the farming. A few families were not strictly tenants but wage hands. One had changed status from tenant to wage hand during the year. The owner gives him a house but no land on which to raise food. As a result they have to spend almost all the wages on food. They plan to remedy this state of affairs next year since the landlord has promised the fifteen-year-old son a few acres to tend on halves. Another wage laborer gets his house and wood and $7 a week, but his thirteen-year-old son has to work for nothing. Several of the share tenants have subtenants from whom they collect one-fourth for supplying a team as does the owner for supplying land. Some of the families changed tenure status during the period of the study. About the same number raised their status through buying a team (usually with the aid of farm security) as lowered their status by losing a team through death, foreclosure, or because they preferred to move to a place where the landlord would rent only on halves.

The modal number of tenants per landowner was reported as one, although it was later learned that Negro tenants often are not counted and some of these should have been put into another classification. In the category of only tenants the families were about equally divided between those where the landowner lived and farmed right on the place and those where the farm had been inherited or bought up as an investment by someone who lived in town. Either case made for modifications in the landlord-tenant relations—the first instance in the direction of a closer association influenced largely by the personality of the landlord, and the second in the direction of no relations at all except the paying of the share at the end of the season. At the other end of the scale, nearly one-sixth of the families lived on plantations having more than twenty tenants. One landlord had fifty-two families on his place, all on contiguous plots and under strict supervision of an overseer; another had sixty scattered in several townships; another, the tenant mother didn't know how many—"they say he owns half of the county."

Regardless of rental shares, the economic returns from farming are so meager that there is a pronounced central tendency about the state of affairs summed up by a mother who said, "If we come out even with all debts paid, we don't complain, and if we have enough money to last till about March, we say we done well." There is as always a range of variation. Two families are reputed to have money in the bank, while one poor family "ain't never come out even except when nobody would credit us."

A few of the women had done something during the year to "bring in a little extry." The most common means of doing this was the stringing of tobacco sacks, which has been described above but which exists no longer. This was one of the ways in which an energetic mother of thirteen earned money during her spare time after caring for her children, cooking, cleaning, sewing, and washing for a family of twelve, working in the field and tobacco barn, hiring out to grade for others when her own crop is stripped, and taking in sewing for nearby owners. Another way is the selling of garden or dairy products, although only one takes her wares regularly to a curb market. One woman says she doesn't like selling in crowds and would rather either sell "straight" or give her extra produce to neighbors. Between stripping barns of their own crop, or after it is finished, a few mothers strip tobacco for other farmers—usually owner-operators who need some extra hands. Or in cotton areas, a few reported hiring out to pick for a few days in the rush season. In any one neighborhood, however, the farms have their rush periods simultaneously and since a tenant usually "tends" as much land as his family can work, the hiring out of women to other farmers is not frequent in this group. One woman and her children hire out as regularly as they can get work now since the husband has pellagra and can no longer farm. Children contributed to the income in about ten percent of the cases. Some few live at home and work in town at mills, restaurants, or ten cent stores. Others get seasonal jobs of the types listed for the fathers or mothers. Jobs are scarce in rural areas, however, and after children leave home to work and live in town, little money is sent back to the farm.

The women's knowledge of the finances of the farm is slightly less exact than their knowledge of its operations because of the absolute control of money matters by the husband, and yet most women knew at least what credit facilities were being used. One explained precisely the rate of interest they pay to a federal land bank after they buy so much stock for each $100 borrowed the first year. Another said her husband has a good name and would rather use it to get regular credit for fertilizer like an owner than to avail himself of lower rates from the government. He prides himself on having paid up voluntarily a back debt when the lien was on only one year's crop and the money couldn't be collected the next year. Another prefers farm security for fertilizer money because if it is a bad year they will not take anything but the crop and you do not lose your team as well. A different attitude is held by one who declared her husband would never again borrow from the government because they kept on sending him letters "six feet long and three feet wide," which he couldn't read, and kept him in a sweat.

The "owner of half the county" furnishes his tenants with fertilizer and credit at a store. He himself told a tenant mother that he had over $30,000 out this year. Those landlords who have stores furnish their tenants with staples, but usually require them to scrape up cash some way or other for school supplies or tobacco. The sharecropper is generally furnished by one method or another if his landlord is solvent, while the share tenant more often arranges his own borrowing. Only two of the whole group had not borrowed or bought on credit this year and one of these is coming out so badly that he has lost his surplus and will have to borrow from the beginning next year. Most of the farm security clients seemed to think this was the best credit source because of lower interest rates. One woman prefers it because she is quite isolated and enjoys the home supervisor's visits while another has stopped using it because she didn't want anyone telling her what to do.

Very few of the families are definitely working toward ownership. One of these has already been described. Another once had money to make a down payment on the place where they live but the owner wouldn't sell it to them. They did not want to buy any other place because they wanted to be near the wife's mother, who has "raised and married" eleven children, all but two of whom live within "what you might call hollering distance." Another family still talk of hoping to own again, but since they lost their farm during the depression they haven't saved a cent any year except what they have paid keeping up insurance on themselves and their children. "Renters are doing mighty well if they break even," the mother explained. Still another family own a small, poor farm which they rent to a man who has a sawmill on it, while they themselves work another man's land on halves in order to have enough acreage for their big family. It seems that there is little actual expectation of the ladder theory working out—materially at least. This seems to make it more urgent to attain recognition and respectability in other ways—by bringing up children properly even if the parents are poor; by insisting that "renters can hold their heads as high as anybody if they live right"; by subscribing to various traditional beliefs as they seek to identify themselves with the economically superior class in their ideology, at least.

On such farms, so financed, so sparing in economic returns, these mothers labor. A considerable amount of field work is not only the modal pattern but is the practice in over three-fourths of the cases. The rule is to do as nearly full-time work as housekeeping and cooking permit during chopping, hoeing, and picking times on the cotton farm, or during most of the summer on the tobacco farm, with the fall spent largely in the striphouse. The number, age, and sex of children make for various modifications in the division of labor. In different families different tasks have priority, but over and above all on tobacco farms is the "saving" or "housing" the crop, that is, priming, stringing, putting into barns, and curing the tobacco. The urgency of this crucial time demands every hand from the youngest child who is able to hand leaves to the oldest grandparent who because of age might be relieved from other field duties. From all other sorts of field work the mother takes off a half day or a day for the weekly washing and sometimes children are excused from field duty to help her. But except where there is, as in one family, a striving for social recognition which keeps daughters out of the field, or, as in another, enough sons so that daughters can be permanently assigned to household tasks, the customary practice is for the father's claim for field work to take precedence over that of the mother for help at the house. This seems to be less a matter of personal dominance than of a recognition of stern economic necessity—by their crops they live and any less urgent matters can wait.

Of the mothers who formerly did field work but do none now except perhaps at saving time, the chief reason for stopping was bad health, although one woman, with an ulcer so bad that she has to hold her stomach with one hand while she worms and suckers tobacco with the other, still works. Another reason for stopping is having produced enough children of full working age who, the mother feels, "take her place." Where there is more than one grown woman in the house—grown daughter, sister, mother, or mother-in-law—there is always an opportunity to divide up work so that one goes to the field and the other stays in the house. This situation was encountered, but more frequently the practice was for both women to work in both places because both preferred field work and neither wished to be confined in the house all day.

In tobacco culture the processes included in the term "stripping"—taking the tobacco off the sticks on which it has been hung for curing and storing, grading it by quality, tying the piles into "hands," and arranging these with final touches for the market—are, strictly speaking, not field work but are done in a house. However, in differentiating between the tasks of homemaking and crop producing, it seems more logical to include them in the category with the other kinds of farm work.

In the striphouse where these processes are carried on, the mother is often the star performer, the chief grader. Although the husband does the directing, decides what lots are to be worked next, assigns tasks to the children, he is usually somewhat respectful of his wife's ability. One mother in a dignified, broad-flapped bonnet gives a truly regal appearance as she presides behind the grading board while her husband and children bring tobacco from the ordering (humidifying) room, take it off sticks, hand it to her, and after she has graded it, tie the piles into neat bundles.

Another can no longer grade because reaching from one end of the board to the other is too hard on her shoulders and chest since she has had pleurisy eight times, and therefore she only ties. However, she is proud of the fact that she can give her husband a two hours' start grading while she cleans house and does all the cooking for the day, and still catch up with him early in the afternoon. The three women of one family count on having to do almost all of the stripping because as the old mother observed from years of experience, "Men ain't no good in 'bacca. They can't set still and work steady. They's always got to be goin' outdoors to see about somp'n—even if they ain't got no excuse better'n the dog." A young mother about seven months pregnant took full responsibility for stripping their crop this fall so that her husband could take a paying job as soon as the tobacco was cured. With some help from her mother-in-law in taking care of her two and four-year-old babies and from her father-in-law with the "ordering," she will finish all their stripping by Thanksgiving. Families sometimes have a barn or two of tobacco left to strip after Christmas if they are not moving at the end of the year. In one case this was explained as intentional in order that they might have some money coming in later after they had spent everything on Santa Claus.

Not only are there the more or less regular operations to be performed on the money crops, cotton and tobacco, but there are many field duties on the food and feed crops considered suitable for women's labor. There are sweet potato vines to be cut before frost, potatoes to be dug later, peas to be picked, fodder to be pulled, and corn to be shucked unless there is a cooperative shucking where only men participate.

In the matter of work preference, an overwhelming majority—seven-eighths—of the mothers like field work (including work in tobacco barns) better than housework. Here again in many instances the statement of preference was annotated with, "I was brought up to it," or "I've always done it." These general statements were sometimes elaborated by descriptions of their bringing up—"We was most all girls and had to do field work just like boys," or contrariwise, "I was the only girl and worked just like a boy with my brothers." There is a great deal of pride in the ability to work like a man, which is evidenced in a boast frequently heard, "My papa said he lost his best hand when I got married." Older women like to reminisce about their former strength. One with pellagra who cannot do field work now because dew or moisture makes her skin crack, bragged of how she had plowed, cut and mauled wood, harrowed, and done everything a man could do before her sons were old enough to work.

The matter of preference was not always so simple. Considering the triple rôle of childbearing and caring, homemaking, and field work, several shared a twenty-year-old mother's view that "If you've got to be taking care of children, too, housework is easier." Her two children give her more trouble in the field than in the house and she has to stop at the end of almost every row to nurse the baby. If it weren't for worrying over them, though, she would rather be working outdoors any time, "because I was brought up that way." Another comment explaining preference occurred so regularly that it could almost be predicted. This was, "In the house you never get through," or a variant, "In the field there's just one thing and you can finish it up; but here in the house there's cooking, cleaning, washing, milking, churning, mending, sewing, canning, and always the children—and you don't know what to turn to next."

There were interesting exceptions in preference. The mother of thirteen who strings tobacco sacks pondered the question seriously, discussed it for several minutes with her husband and children, and finally gave a joint report that she liked washing best of all. She always had liked it and now, since she has a gasoline engine washer, she is sure she loves washing most of all—and next to that stripping tobacco. A few husbands prefer their wives to keep the children at home out of the way in the field. These women and a few others prefer work indoors. One mother who claimed this preference because she "wasn't brought up to work in the field," had her statement pooh-poohed by her husband who said she knew she liked stripping tobacco and working with him best.

This last remark suggests the enjoyment of companionship in field and barn which only a few mentioned explicitly but which many were observed to be enjoying. The work in the striphouse is favorable to conversation and tall tale telling. One daughter yelled, "You all shut up!" to several women working inside as the visitor approached a striphouse. They later confessed they had been telling "mighty rough jokes." In several places a nephew, brother-in-law, grown son, or other relative was helping a man and his wife with stripping and the three were laughing or joking as the visitor came in. The cotton farm mother does not have such a good opportunity for combining sociability with work, although cotton picking is usually done in groups. One mother who does not have to pick now goes to the field with her young children since they enjoy it more and pick better when they are all out together. Still another reason for preference of field and barn work given by old timers is the "smell of 'bacca." One woman sniffed audibly and said, "Just smell it and you'll see why all my children except the two who stay in the house chew—boys and girls."

To the question of preference an older woman answered somewhat regretfully, "Housework now, I guess, I just can't hold out any more in the field, though I used to work like a man." Age and failing health abate zest and enthusiasm for the preferred outdoor work. Even the mother whose interests are so centered in farming, after she had declared she had always liked field work best, sighed and added, "But I gets mighty tired now—and there's never no rest."

Chapter 8

Of Housekeeping

THE TENANT farm mother's work—which is most of her life—may be classified into three sorts of activities: bearing and caring for children; housekeeping—including all other phases of homemaking; and actual farming. The first two classes are often treated together but are here considered separately, since each is certainly a sizable job in itself. Of all these duties, housekeeping makes the most regular demands. Farm work varies with the seasons from almost full time to none at all, the burden of childbearing and caring shifts with time, but housekeeping—cooking, cleaning, washing, sewing—goes on forever. The assignment by custom of this phase of family responsibility to woman is no more questioned on tenant farms than the assignment of the bearing of children to her by nature. "Woman's place" may be enlarged to include the field, but this expansion of realm does not diminish her obligations of service in the house.

The house, which is the locus of this type of work, may be described in terms of a few modal traits. Such a composite house is an unpainted, one-story, weatherboard structure of four rooms. It is without electricity, running water, radio, or phonograph, but does have a sewing machine and inadequate screens. There are a few scattered flowers in the front yard, but no grass. The porch steps and floor are badly in need of repair. Cracks under the doors let in icy drafts in winter. The front sitting-bedroom has curtains and, for decoration, calendars on the wall and photographs on the mantel.

In spite of the existence of these modal traits, variation

from them was so frequent and great that there was little suggestion of uniformity. An important basis of differentiation was whether the house had been built for tenants or for owners as this affected both size and quality of construction. About one-fourth of the houses had been built for owners, yet often their age and lack of upkeep offset their better original quality. In size the houses ranged from eight two-room cabins to five of more than eight rooms. In the larger houses sometimes as few as three rooms were used for living and often one or more rooms were used for storage for the tenant or the owner or for tobacco stripping. The size of family frequently failed to correspond to the size of the house. One family of twelve lived in three rooms while a couple without children at home occupied a house of four rooms. Many of the bedrooms in which the visits took place had two double beds in them, indicating silently the lack of privacy. Kitchen and dining room were always one and sometimes served as bedrooms also. Some of the smaller houses as well as the larger had rooms sacrificed for tobacco stripping and storage during the fall.

The older houses showed more attention to design while those constructed within the last twenty-five years had little architectural beauty. The most humble but most picturesque type of the former consisted of one main room of log with a stoop in front, a half-story sleeping loft above, and a shed kitchen behind. Eleven of the sixteen houses visited in one county were of log and of this general type although some of them had more rooms. The interior walls of such log houses and the hearth to the fireplace are often whitewashed with white mud from local deposits. The larger types of older houses vary from modest, unpretentious, "rambling" houses with ells to a two-story, colonial type with columns. The newer houses built for tenants were rarely attractive and were more often of the boxlike variety. Several were converted into dwellings from other structures—a schoolhouse, a filling station, or a tourist cabin.

The general condition of repair was truly good in only a very few cases. Where porches were present, the most noticeable defects were almost universally rotting or broken porch steps and floors. Although one-third of the houses had been painted formerly, only a few were freshly painted. One was a prerevolutionary home which the manager's wife assured me was being kept up to preserve it for the absentee owners—"not for the sake of those people who live in it—they don't appreciate it." Illustrative evidences of misuse and bad upkeep were pencil markings covering the front of one house, window sashes knocked out from unused upper stories, broken window panes, torn screens, holes in floors, a door which fell to pieces when opened. Three of the houses are said to be over a hundred years old—the one which is well kept by the owners and two others so long neglected that sloping floors, plastering falling off walls, and an atmosphere of decay did much to ruin the charm of the fine wide boards in the flooring and wainscoting. Not confined to the oldest houses were cracks of an inch or more under doors or in worn floors, caused in some cases by careless construction and in others by lack of repair, which were responsible for keeping feet like icicles during winter visits. Drabness and bad repair were the mode, but there was a spick-and-spanness to the exterior of one house which was partly surrounded with neatly painted, trim barns and outhouses. Another family during a one year's stay managed to give to an old, weather-beaten, two-story house the appearance of being kept up by having the yards and porches in perfect order with tidiness evident in every arrangement, by tacking screen wire over all the windows, and hanging screen doors at the front and back.

The scarcity of grass lawns is explicable in some cases by

the presence of good shade trees, which make grass growing difficult. There were flowers in many more instances either in the front, back, or side yard, or in pots on the porches. Shrubs planted with an eye to symmetry were rarer. The yards generally had the earmarks of utilitarian rather than esthetic virtues. Functionally, the back yard is the juncture of field and home, the place where teams are hitched, plows and implements left, the dinner bell rung, chickens fed, cotton unloaded. The back yard is more constantly used than any other area—the front door is often locked and even visitors have to come and go by way of the back yard; the water drawer, the milker, and the feeder of stock traverse it several times a day; and all members of the family cross it on the way to and from the privy, if there is one. Artificial beautifying would be out of place and the cluttered appearance, due to wagons, harrows, saw horses, wash pots, clothes lines, chicken coops, tools, and sundry odds and ends, is to be expected.

The tenant can do little about the gross aspects of his physical surroundings. The possibility of having to move at the end of any year makes any considerable expenditure for paint or carpentering unwise, even if he could afford it. Since housing is one of the things "handed down from above," it is accepted with a certain degree of equanimity. One woman's present house is not so good as the one she had before but the land is better and "that's the way it is—there are good points and bad points to every place." Furthermore, she knows that the landowner, who is her nearest neighbor, can't afford to spend anything on it because he doesn't make much more than the tenants do. Another mother who has lived in a much better home thinks hers is in a terrible state, but their landowner is paralyzed and she doesn't want to worry him about it. While one complained of not enough room, another regretted that they were about to move into a six-room house which her furniture and family of six couldn't begin to fill up. Still another anticipated with great delight a move to a brand new house for her daughter's sake. An exceptional mother, interrupted while painting the walls of her front bedroom, blames the conditions of tenant houses on the tenants themselves. She thinks that if all of them did as she does, "One would reap where another had sowed," and all would be better off. She enumerated the various improvements she had made in a half-dozen houses in which she had lived. She will not let her husband rent a place until she has inspected the house. Much more frequent, however, were women who were planning to move in a few weeks to houses, often not more than a mile or two away, which they had never seen, or at least had never entered.

All the interiors were not seen since many visits took place in the striphouse, on the porch, in the yard, or in the field. Even when the visit was inside, often only one room could be observed, since the inspection of houses was secondary to establishing rapport with the mother. In those seen, the furniture can quickly be inventoried: in the kitchen a wood stove or range, an oilcloth-covered table for preparing food and for eating, and a safe for storing and keeping food were standard equipment with work table, china closet, cabinet, or sideboard occasionally; in the sitting-bedroom one or two double beds, a sewing machine more often than not, a dresser, and several chairs drawn up around the fireplace or stove constituted the necessities, with now and then a radio, victrola, organ, or center table. A portable item is the cradle, which may be found in the kitchen, striphouse, bedroom, or wherever the mother may be working. Scarcity of furniture was sometimes explained by accounts of having been "burnt out," while rarely found bedroom or living room suites of furniture were generally ascribed to former periods of relative prosperity usually when the mother or father was working in the mill.

There were many examples of ingenuity in both decorative and useful articles. One mother had pieced together flour sacks for curtains and embroidered the valances attractively with colored thread, while her husband had made a fly proof, kiddie-coop type of baby bed by hand. One had draped with multicolored bunting a gilt framed picture, another had sprinkled pines with whitewash for Christmas decoration. Another had curtained a corner neatly with cretonne to make a closet, and another displayed with pride a room she had just papered herself. Sons had built homemade checker boards to be used with bottle caps, benches, and baby pens. Pieced quilts were used for spreads as often as cotton or rayon ones. A woman who does no field work had made very pretty, tiny ones to fit her baby's cradle. There were several embroidered scarfs on dressers and sewing machines, occasionally cut flowers—once in a beer bottle—and about as often, cheap, artificial tulips or roses.

Interiors, however, were usually characterized by a lack of color and by drabness. This sensory deprivation in the lives of developing children is illustrative of the general cultural lacks in their environment. In one home a bright, talkative, four-year-old child insisted on showing his scant store of treasures—one of them a small Sears Roebuck sales catalogue. He liked best the page of it which contained a color chart for house paint. He asked the names of the colors and in a few minutes learned four or five of them. He proved his knowledge by locating the colors on the visitor's dress which had flecks of various hues. Then, anxious to exhibit his newly acquired knowledge on broader fields, he began looking around the room for other colors to identify. He scanned all the clothes hanging around the wall, his mother's dress, the two pieced quilts on the bed, but nowhere was there even a tiny spot one could still call color —only the faded near-gray which is the common fate of all colors. He shook his head sadly as he reported on his survey, "We ain't got no colors." In another home where there were four young children, the only literature or printed matter of any sort was a highway map obtained from a filling station. One of the children demonstrated his ability to read on this map, for he had no school books.

The standard decoration was calendars with every variety of pictures adorning them and of past years quite as often as of the current. Some sitting-bedrooms had more than a dozen each of these. Second only to calendars were pictures of members of the family with the place of honor given to those who had died. In one home there was a what-not full of photographs and a whole album of snapshots of the children. The walls of a theologically minded mother were dignified with religious pictures and in her home alone did the Holy Bible rest imposingly on the center table.

To one accustomed to closets and cupboards the most striking feature of the interiors is that all possessions are exposed. Clothes are hung on nails around the walls and shoes are suspended by their heels along the top edge of a mirror or molding. An unused baby bed may be piled high with odds and ends and in the more provident households jars of fruit and vegetables line the walls of the hall or are stacked in corners of bedroom and kitchen. Guns, hatchets, and other useful tools as well as extravagantly-dressed dolls from fairs, hornets' nests, and dried animal skins are held up by nails in the walls. The absence of enclosed storage space is probably the most noticeable lack of what we call "modern conveniences" but perhaps not the most important. Only eight of the homes had electricity—in an area considered progressive in rural electrification—and not a single one had running water. The extra work required to fill and clean kerosene lamps, draw and carry water, empty chambers and slop jars is hard to imagine—as one mother put it bluntly, "Town folks just don't know." Where there was electricity, it was used for lights, radio, and ironing, but in only two cases for power appliances, such as washing machines and refrigerators. In two homes where electricity was quite new, all members of the family were very enthusiastic over it and vowed they would go without anything else to pay the three-dollar-a-month minimum charge. The water supply was most often a well, although quite a few families were without even this and had to carry all water used from a spring or neighbor's well sometimes as far as a half mile away.

Of the various divisions of housekeeping, housecleaning is the most open to inspection and sizing up by a visitor. All degrees of orderliness were observed and although there was no rating made of these, there seemed to be a positive correlation of degree of orderliness with the number of adult females in the home and a negative one with the number of small children. A mother with four children under school age had the dirtiest, most disorderly house imaginable. Shoes, underwear, and an axe were on the kitchen table along with uncovered food left from dinner. The floor was strewn with varied litter and dirt. In the kitchen two boys chased each other under the high-legged stove and up the pile of wood behind, scattering still another layer of bark, chips, and potato peelings over the room. In contrast, another woman's front bedroom was so neat and dustless that it would have done credit to a New England housewife. In the middle range the beds were usually made—sometimes with dirty quilts, but still made—the floor was clean except where children were playing at the moment, clothes were hung on the corners of beds or backs of chairs, but hung and not lying around. In the kitchen the table was almost never cleared, but food dishes were covered either separately with overturned plates or together with a tablecloth.

Any evaluation of the results of housecleaning efforts should take into consideration the mother's knowledge and training, implements, space, and the presence of children quickly undoing whatever straightening she might finish. Lack of knowledge of the essentials of sanitation was evident in one mother's care of her log house. She had dug white mud from the banks of a branch and whitewashed the mud-chinked log walls. She had recently scrubbed the wide board floors with sand, since she had no soap. The floor boards were beautiful —almost white, it was revealed when a child walking across the room dispersed the flies, which had formed almost a solid coating. That such hard-earned cleanliness was polluted with literally millions of flies was a telling indication of the mother's ignorance of relative values. Another factor to be remembered is the time demands of field work. Because she has so little time and energy left after working outdoors most of the day, one mother says, "I just *smear* up instead of cleaning up." Still another factor is the modal preference for outdoor work which brought forth statements such as, "No woman really likes housework," and "I used to tell my mother, 'Don't tell me to do nothing in the house; let me work in the field.' "

"Broomsage" brooms are the only kind in many of the homes and some women prefer them. There were no floor mops visible, although the condition of the unpainted floors usually testified to frequent scrubbings. There was linoleum in several kitchens and bedrooms and a very few small rugs; but floor coverings of any kind were most infrequent. A kitchen visit was interrupted several times when the mother left to chase a pig out of the next room where he came in through an unscreened door to root a ragged matting carpet. The lightening of housekeeping caused by the scarcity of possessions to be kept straight and by the smallness of the establishment seems to be outbalanced by the lack of modern aids. The old-fashioned back-breaking ways of doing things prevail and "straightening" must be done continually because practically all of the belongings have to remain "out."

Even more time consuming is cooking. Factors increasing the time differential between tenant farm and urban cooking are wood stoves with fires to be built and kept going, correspondingly old-fashioned implements, larger size of families to be fed, bigger appetites of outdoor workers, the preparing of raw materials from scratch rather than using expensive, bought, semi-prepared foods, and dietary preferences which demand hot bread at every meal, home baked pies and cakes, and vegetables cooked for many hours. One mother cooks for nine on a small, high-legged, wood stove; another who cooks for twelve cuts her own wood as well as builds her fires; another cooks ninety biscuits twice a day and uses a barrel of flour every two weeks; another cooks for two field hands besides her own family; many have dogs to feed—sometimes as many as a half dozen; and only a few have anything so modern as a pressure cooker. The hours of meals spread cooking and dishwashing over almost the entire span of working hours. "Before light" breakfasts and "after dark" suppers, twelve o'clock dinners, packing school lunches, and feeding the children again when they return in the afternoon are the customary pattern.

From conversational interviews it is almost impossible to get exact information on diet. Certain dietary habits have been practiced for so many years that they are not reported explicitly since the mother assumes anyone would take them for granted. For instance, the lack of fat meat for seasoning vegetables is one of the most frequently cited hardships of a current or previous "bad year," yet no mother in describing her ways of cooking stated expressly that she used fat meat in cooking vegetables. Only a young woman with a nonrural, out-of-state background could give a summary description of her meals on a relative basis: here they have bigger breakfasts; dinners in the middle of the day, of course, consisting of as many vegetables as their garden provides, no separately cooked meat, corn pones, and always something sweet, "like [sweet] potato pudding"; suppers of left over vegetables, hot biscuits, and meat when they can afford it.

The modal Sunday dinner can be described better because it is different. It always features a meat—chicken, beef, fresh pork, or cheese, which is rated as much a luxury as meat because it must be bought. It also has the more preferred fresh or canned vegetables—"snaps," butterbeans (small lima beans), or cabbage—and sometimes extra things like soup, apple sauce, or tomatoes. The dessert may be cake—"Cake, of course," said one mother—or pie or pudding. Some of the hardest up have no different meal on Sunday. If a certain mother has a chicken to spare, she kills it during the week so that her children may have some of it for school lunches, which are her greatest problem since so often, "there ain't nothing to send except baked potatoes." The traditional Southern pattern of overflowing tables with many sorts of meats simply does not exist in this group. Only once were two meats listed for one meal, "Ham and chicken because of the preacher, you know," said a woman who had invited the minister for the fourth Sunday. On the other hand, meals of only cabbage, sweet potatoes, or field peas were actually eaten on the days of visits, sometimes because there was nothing else on hand and no money to buy with, sometimes because the mother could not leave the striphouse in the middle of the day to cook more. During the stripping season one mother's practice is common among the women who have no grown daughters to do the cooking while they are working. If it is not too cold, she cooks up some bread and vegetables in the morning while she is fixing breakfast and at twelve o'clock they go to the house and eat them cold—and hurriedly for there has been no fire in the house for several hours and tenants' homes cool off almost instantaneously. Or if it is a very cold day, she leaves the striphouse about eleven-thirty, builds a fire in the kitchen stove, and "fries up somp'n in a hurry."

The results of the diet in hard years were sometimes visible. A twelve-year-old son who has had both pellagra and rickets looks no more than eight now. When the doctors and nurses asked his mother, "What *have* you been feeding him?" she told them she was glad none of her family had glass stomachs so people could see what had gone in them. This was a year when they could not even farm because they had lost all their stock and were not able to find any landlord who would furnish them. Another sighed as she admitted that while her ten children are in good health, they all look mighty puny except one. This was so true that when they came in from school and the field, they could not be identified from the age listing given in advance because each was nearly twice as old as he looked.

Only one out of seven of the families had no cow. One family had six, two of which, a little girl of ten bragged, were pure-bred Jerseys which were going to be registered. The possession of a cow, however, does not always insure adequate milk consumption. If there is only one, which is the modal number, she will be dry for a part of each year and it depends on the particular neighborhood whether sharing prevails to the extent that a family is "never without milk," as some reported. Another reason is not unique to tenant or rural families—that some children will simply not drink milk. An even more common reason is the lack of adequate feed for the cow. Another reason, given by two families who do not let their children drink milk, is the belief that sweet milk makes children wormy.

The year's canning ranged from none at all in a fourth of the families to over five hundred quarts in several, with "we put up a right smart, but not enough to last through the winter," as the mode. Mention of canning usually called forth a comment upon the ravages of the beetle, which has in many areas completely ruined the beans and affected other plants in recent years, cutting down the supply of fresh vegetables in summer as well as that of canned ones in winter. The next most common complaint was that there were no fruit trees or even berries on the place. The process of "putting up" is done with the most simple equipment. It is called "canning" although glass jars are used rather than cans. Since the canning season coincides with the time for summer field work, much of it is done at night or before breakfast. Soup mixture, tomatoes, and beans lead the list. The cost of sugar limits preserving and jellying of fruits and berries. When the difficulties of time, materials, and equipment are surmounted, the store of canned goods forms one of the chief sources of pride to the housewife. "Excuse me for changing the subject, but look what I got put up for the winter," said one mother as she led the way through her kitchen, the corners of which were overflowing to the center of the room with quart jars. Many a woman when speaking of canning added, "and I didn't have a single one to spoil last winter," or "I've never lost but two quarts of tomatoes," impressive records when one considers that only a very few of them were members of home demonstration clubs or had any notions of applied bacteriology. Since most of the homes have no cellars, the jars are stored in kitchens or bedrooms, which are heated, to prevent freezing.

It is generally conceded that of all the housekeeping tasks, washing is the heaviest and hardest. Here were the only instances in which the mothers had any hired help: in two cases where a colored woman came in once a week to assist with the washing for a few hours, in two cases where it was sent out to a washerwoman, and in one case where the overalls and sheets were sent to a laundry. The scarcity of clothing and linens makes weekly washing the rule, with deviations all on the side of greater frequency. Here again the job is bigger and harder than in town, so much so that a mother is very likely to have help from her husband or children—at least in cutting wood, making a fire under the pot in the yard, and drawing water. Women almost always mention the overalls; scrubbing clean a pair that has been worn a week for farm work requires so much effort that it can not be taken for granted, even though it is routine. The other critical point in washing is baby diapers. If the baby only wets them, they are often simply dried without being washed. When hung before the fire from the mantel or on chairs, the odor is suffused throughout the room. The soiled diapers must be washed, though, and this was designated as the most distasteful task oftener than any other.

The usual amount of sewing done is the mother's own clothes, her baby's, and some for her daughters. Some do none at all, and one makes all her family's wearing apparel except overalls, even shirts for her two-hundred-and-fifty-pound husband. Quite a few mentioned a decrease in sewing since children's clothes can be bought more cheaply now. Most of them sew without patterns, cutting by copying or by guess. They are interested in materials and several offered information as to where one can buy ends, remnants, and seconds from nearby mills. And yet not one mother in all the visits ever made a comment or asked a question about styles as such, except for deploring the immoral designs of bathing suits and shorts. There is a long time between new dresses and, since keeping in style is financially impossible, it is not a matter of great interest.

A job somewhat intermediate between housework and farm work is the care of the stock. As a rule the husband feeds the mules and pigs and the wife feeds the chickens and cow and does the milking. There is often a shift from this as children get older and either sons or daughters relieve the parents. Bad health in one case and seven small children in another explain the husband's having taken over the milking. The two oldest women think, "a man just can't handle a cow right," and several claimed their cows would not "let down" their milk for a man. The devotion of the women to the animals they care for sometimes approaches that for their children. An ordinarily undemonstrative woman talks to her cow, which she has raised herself, all the time she is milking her and the cow often looks back at the woman "like she understood." The disciplinary measures necessary when another was weaning a calf hurt her more than whipping a child. At one home there was a joyful greeting with the news that the cow had "come in" since the last visit. One woman just won't sell a pet calf for veal. She knows the calf will make a good milker like her mother and she prefers to give her away to someone who will keep her. When the State Fair was mentioned, the things the mothers most often expressed a wish to see were the poultry and cattle. Whether the feeding and milking are done by the mother or by someone else, the straining of the milk and the lifting of pans and churns are almost always her job. Although a child may do the actual churning, supervising this process and finally working up the butter complete the mother's round of dairy products chores.

Children usually help in many of the housekeeping tasks described, but during the first ten or fifteen years of marriage, it is probably safe to estimate that as much time must be given to the training of children as is saved by their work. And even when several children are old enough to give considerable help, the mother must still keep the responsibility for planning, directing, and articulating the work of each to keep things running smoothly. Another adult woman in the family, mother, mother-in-law, spinster, or widowed sister or daughter affords the greatest help, of course.

At any rate the work is sufficient to keep the women going all day. Few reported ever resting during the daytime—one who is trying to prevent another miscarriage, another who considers herself frail, another since she has had pneumonia. The wish for rest was freely admitted by several to be one reason for giving a cordial welcome. "I like *any* kind of company because it gives me an excuse to stop and rest," said one who insisted upon leaving her work and entertaining the visitor in the front bedroom. The visitor's reaction to their housekeeping is one of surprise, not that their meals are unbalanced or their homes somewhat untidy, but that they are able to keep up the level of energy output during almost every waking hour, day in and day out, year after year, which is demanded for getting big families fed, cleaned after, washed and sewed for, with such meager and inadequate equipment, and with such antiquated methods.

Chapter 9

Of Childbearing

HERE WE COME to the part of the tenant mother's life which is of crucial interest to the student of population. We do not minimize the importance of her field work and farming, which are closely tied up with erosion, land tenure, marketing, and other problems for the agronomist or agricultural economist; nor her housekeeping and cooking, which are a challenge to the home economist and dietician; but the producing and rearing of children so prodigiously as to exceed replacement needs and to supply a store for other occupations, communities, and regions is her function which is of primary concern to us.

Before going to the case material illustrative of this functioning, we present a brief, quantitative summary of fertility characteristics within the group visited. These figures are not used as a basis for generalizations on the fertility of all tenant farm mothers, but are offered to indicate the level of this particular group. It is a sector of the overlapping area of the highest fertility classes of all, save one, of the categories by which fertility differentials are customarily analyzed: i.e. by race, region, socio-economic class, and size of community. We assume that the high reproductive rate of mothers in the Southeastern Region, of those in the lowest socio-economic class, and of those who live on rural farms has been established with sufficient validity by studies treating primarily of quantitative indices. Quantitative data are used here simply to identify the group from whom qualitative information on the operation of fertility patterns has been taken.

Of the 129 mothers visited in the Subregion, complete an

usable records on age, age at marriage, duration of marriage, and number and age of children are compiled for only 117. Ten of the other 12 were found to be small owners, incorrectly referred to as tenants, and two moved before complete information was secured. Of the 117 tenant farm mothers, the 115 married mothers have been married a total of 2,175 years, or an average of 18.9 years. Since some of them are over 45, some have had various types of sterilization, and others have been or are now widows, their total years of exposure to pregnancy during marriage are 1,979, or an average of 17.2 years. During this time they have borne 740 live children, of whom 634 are still living. The mean number of children borne per married mother is 6.4, and the mean number of children borne per year of exposure to pregnancy during marriage is 0.37, or an average of one child for each period of a little less than three years. Any birth rate based upon data for women who have not yet completed the childbearing period is higher than the true one for the whole span, but the number of women here does not justify a more elaborate computation by the method of age specific fertility rates. If a woman married at the age of 18.6, the mean age at marriage of this group, and exhibited the above rate until she was 45, she would bear 10 children. This estimate is too high because of the inclusion of more years of the earlier higher fertility period than of the later in computing the rate. We may note, however, that since the median age of the mothers is 39, for half of them a part or all of the less fertile years in the later period are included.

The mean number of children borne per woman is 6.3, but because of the weighting effect of large families, over two-thirds of the children are in families where there are seven or more children. These figures do not include stillbirths or abortions because information on them was secured from only about half the mothers and even the information secured was not considered very reliable. The women reporting had an average of about 0.5 pregnancy other than those resulting in live births.

In spacing of children, there is almost invariably an increase in length of time between successive births as the mother becomes older. The modal pattern is a baby about every two years for a while, then longer and longer intervals up to six, 10 or, in one case, 15 years. Many instances were reported of closer spacing: a young mother had two babies by the time she had been married a little more than a year and a half; another, married at 13, was left a widow with five children at the age of 24; another, whose husband had had nine children by his first wife, had 12 by the time she was 36; another, married at 16, had 12 at 37; another had 16 born singly at 40; and another had three sets of twins and seven born singly by the age of 41. On the other hand, there were mothers who had been married for many years who had only one, two, or three children.

It is evident from the data presented that this group is one of high fertility in which childbearing is a matter of great importance both to the mother and to society. We attempt now to describe some of the attitudes and practices relating to this significant function.

Pregnancy, or "when I was 'that way' with my oldest," is a time about which the mothers relish telling. But, as in the case with diet, the routine—for it actually becomes that with these mothers—is often taken for granted, and the particular pregnancies where the mother was sickest or had the greatest trouble of one sort or another are usually the ones singled out for the most thorough description. The practice regarding pregnancies most frequently reported by the mothers and most emphasized with specific accounts is that they worked "right on up to the last." "I helped house the crop up through the very evening that John was born that night," and "I did all my week's washing the morning I was took sick when my fifth come—it was a Tuesday," were repeated with slight variations again and again. Mothers visited during pregnancy were usually found at their customary tasks—stripping tobacco, washing, scrubbing floors, cooking. Only one was modifying her regimen by resting and having her washing done to prevent a miscarriage.

Almost every mother described the birth of a child, varying in fullness of detail according to the presence or absence of children and their age and sex. It was often interesting to notice the immediate shifting to the biological and especially to the obstetrical features the moment a husband or child left the room and there was privacy. Older women took the precaution of inquiring about marital status. An affirmative reply to, "Air you a married woman?" assured them on this point and the relationship became more nearly one of equals in the discussion of this subject. Childbirth is regarded as an achievement for which the tenant mother need make no apologies as she might for housekeeping or her children's clothes. There is more often than not a touch of pride in her voice as she relates her experiences in "having a baby." Lines of class distinction vanish in sharing reminiscences about this most fundamental of realities. Upon hearing that the visitor had only one child and that with little difficulty, one woman could not restrain herself: "Then you don't know *nothing* about having babies—you just listen to *me*. I 'granny' for all the women around here. . . ." With gusto she continued accounts of general practices interspersed with vivid illustrations from her own experience and that of other women she had "grannied" for.

The place of childbirth is the home, occasionally that of the mother's or father's parents for the first child, or rarely the hospital. This means interrupting the household routine in several ways. First, the other children must be disposed of for the actual duration of labor. The most common practice is sending them off to their grandmother's or their aunt's or a neighbor's. As soon as one mother felt the first pain, she would rush with the children down the road about a quarter of a mile to her mother-in-law's, leave them there, and hurry back with the mother-in-law, who was a "granny." Speed was necessary because she was never in labor more than an hour except once. Another who took much longer could pack up her children's things more leisurely and have her husband take them off to a relative's for a few days' visit when she decided it was time for him to go for the doctor. Seven of another's eight children were born at night and so all she had to do was to move the children back into the kitchen and let them go on sleeping. Another can't bear to have her children sleep away from her and has never sent them off. When she had to be taken to the hospital for an instrumental delivery of her baby, now two months old, she insisted on coming home the next day to be with her children, even though it meant having an ambulance.

Next there must be an arrangement made for someone to take over the housekeeping and cooking duties for a week or so after the child is born while the mother is in bed. This function designated as "staying with" is not to be confused with "grannying" which means assisting during the actual birth process, although sometimes the same person may do both. In a few cases the families could afford to hire someone, usually a Negro woman. The customary practice, however, is for some female relative—mother, sister, niece, mother-in-law, sister-in-law, or cousin—to come and take charge of the housework and of the care of the children for a week or two for no pay. It is more often done by an older woman whose children are grown, by the family spinster, or by a fairly young woman not yet married. Practicing mothers cannot leave their families for so long a time. Thus this usually unpaid service is not on an exchange basis, but is something that those without children can and are expected to do for the childbearers. If there is a daughter over fourteen at home, the girl often can manage without outside help. In poorer families who have moved far away from relatives, the husband may have to take over these tasks. In several such cases reported, the wife gets up too early in order to relieve him. One husband who used to cook on a railroad doesn't mind the cooking; they let the housekeeping go, and the Negro "granny" comes back every day to bathe the new baby.

Eighty-five percent of the children of these mothers were delivered by doctors, but several mothers had never had doctors and several others had had them only for the first child. When a midwife is employed she is paid $5 to $10 for her services during labor, birth, and for a few hours afterwards. There her duties end unless there is an overlapping of the "grannying" and the "staying with" functions. Midwives are usually Negroes now, although one woman's mother and mother-in-law were both "regular grannies." The qualifying adjective, "regular," may technically connote "licensed," but in ordinary usage it distinguishes midwives, who deliver babies alone, from non-professional women, as often white as Negro, who are not licensed and who do not actually deliver except in an emergency, but who go to assist the doctor and to perform the duties of a nurse under his supervision. Such women "granny" but are not "regular grannies" and usually receive no pay, although sometimes they get presents.

The doctor who "birthed" all of one woman's own children, all her mother's nine, and all her sister's thirteen sends for this woman to come whenever he has a hard case, even when she does not know the woman who is being delivered. She told the doctor she thought she'd begin charging, too, it took so much of her time—but this was proposed jokingly as if the very idea were preposterous. She says "grannying" upsets her because she is nervous, but she feels it's something that has to be done and it's one time when a woman needs all the help she can get from anybody. She heats water, gives chloroform, holds the woman's hands if she needs help when she's "bearing down," hands the doctor things, bathes and dresses the baby, and helps clean up after the birth. She has never actually cut the cord although the doctor has shown her just how to do it if necessary. She leaves when the doctor does, but sometimes they send for her to come back instead of going for the doctor again if the navel starts bleeding or if they have some other trouble afterwards. Sometimes a regular midwife performs these services under a doctor's supervision, in which case she is paid. Sometimes a colored woman who is not a "regular granny" is used as a practical nurse and paid. The most frequent practice, however, is for some white neighbor who can "granny" to come and help. Even a busy mother can lay down her work for a half day or so to help another.

Several mothers had borne children with no help because the doctor or midwife did not get there in time. A woman's sixth baby was born one night after the worst snow storm in years. She had always used midwives, but there was none around in that community—it was just four miles from town. Her husband walked to town to get the doctor after they put the children back in the kitchen. Because of the snow and a crust on it which broke through, the doctor could not get any nearer than the highway in his car and had to find a mule to ride on for the last mile and a half. The baby had been born a half hour when he and the husband finally arrived. The mother had been all alone so she just covered the newborn baby with a quilt and without cutting the cord let it lie there until the doctor came. Having babies alone is a fast fading practice, but, if we go back a generation, many can tell of their mothers' experiences—several of whom preferred having them while sitting on slop jars instead of lying in bed. One woman's mother had a doctor with her first and watched everything he did very carefully. After that she always had her own alone. She wouldn't even let a neighbor woman come in to "granny" because she didn't like having anybody around. She would call her husband in when she wanted him to hand her things. She had ten children and learned the art of delivery so well on herself that "after nature left her," she started "regular grannying." Although she is nearly eighty now, she helped one young girl this fall.

In describing labor and the actual process of giving birth, the points featured are those to which some pride in achievement can be attached. The duration of labor is a matter where either extreme seems to be a basis for prestige. One mother with an air of condescension and pity for her weaker sisters claimed, "I *never* took over a few hours except with my first, and this knee-baby, here, was born in less than a half hour." Another described almost hour by hour nearly a week of labor with the implication that only a courageous person could have lived through it. The one who "grannies" said anyone can stand a day of being in labor; it's on the second and third and fourth days when you're "plum wore out" and "feel like you can't do nothing else" that you wish you could die and don't see how you can stand it. She went so long with one of hers that her arms and hands couldn't "hold out no longer." When she simply couldn't grip under the bed, her husband would come sit near and hold her wrists for her. Those whose labor was of normal duration—from four to twelve or twenty-four hours—did not dwell upon its rehearsal as did the ones who either got through quickly or who took a very long time.

The other bragging point is in not yelling. One explained

that she could keep her children right in the house because she never "carried on." Another says she always "grunted it out" with no other noise. One shamefacedly confessed to weakness in this respect although she justified herself by claiming that anyone would have to holler that went through what she did. One woman telling of a spoiled sister with implied condemnation said she screamed so loud that her children, who were nearly a mile away, heard her. "Grannies" naturally dislike the noise and are probably responsible for originating two superstitious beliefs about yelling which were found in almost every neighborhood visited. One is that if you yell on a pain, you will have to have it over again; the other is that if you yell too loud and too much, you will kill the baby. Admonitions regarding this last one are often effective in silencing the mother when nothing else will. Some mothers object to having a certain "granny" because she puts her hand over their mouths and stops them from yelling.

Lacerations, hemorrhoids, and dislocated uterus are among the most frequently reported after effects of childbearing. In most cases the doctor does not come back after the delivery if the tenant home is a long way out of town. The lack of medical attention to these ailments is almost universal, perhaps because of no money to pay the doctor, perhaps because of a reticence about examination for female troubles. One woman "split right straight from one opening to the other" after her third child every time another was born—and she has eleven. Twice she has been sewed by a reputable gynecologist. However, she tears right open again the next time and she has decided that she just won't go through with the sewing up again until she knows she will not be pregnant any more. She is forty-two now and so it won't be many more years. Another has suffered from piles for twenty-one years since her first child was born. It gets worse with every succeeding one and sometimes gets her down when she overworks, but she has never gone to a doctor about it. An older woman's womb fell when her tenth child was born nearly thirty years ago, but she has never wanted a doctor to examine her.

Some of the common superstitions about prenatal influences were encountered. One mother is sure her harelipped child was marked one Sunday in church when she stared at her husband's cousin's harelipped boy, although she "swears 'fore God" she didn't mock him. ("Mark" and "mock" are pronounced very much alike and this coupled with the close causal relation between the two makes understanding difficult. The belief is that if a mother "mocks" an afflicted person, she "marks" the child she is carrying with the same affliction.) Another belief is that crawling through fences or narrow places makes the cord wrap around the baby's head and choke it to death. When one baby was born like this the mother-in-law said accusingly, "I told you about climbing through that fence," and completely upset the mother about killing the baby. Another woman who suffered from insomnia during pregnancy is sure this is why her baby sleeps so little now. Another whose husband died while she was pregnant thinks this is the reason her youngest child mopes all the time.

Closely associated with superstitions are strange bits of misinformation about physiology and anatomy. A mother who had a four-year wait between two of her children said that her "womb closed right back up like before the first was born" and she had just as hard a time as with her first. She told her husband it was certainly easier to have them close together. Another claims that a ball the size of your fist in her "privy" is caused from the muscles breaking loose from her stomach and falling down. Another mother who had two children just fourteen months apart following the extraction of all her teeth attributed causal significance to the lack of teeth. In embarrassment over two children so close together, she told the doctor it would have been cheaper to get plates. The old idea of nursing preventing another pregnancy was often referred to, but most of the mothers have lost faith in it from empirical observation. Often they know "it just ain't true" from personal experience. There were a number of reports of "getting catched before I started back." Another belief indirectly alluded to but only once expressly stated is that a woman conceives when she has an orgasm. Several stated, "It's not my fault that I have so many children—I never enjoyed it one bit," or "I never could tell when they started—it didn't feel a bit different like they said it would."

"Blue babies" were often mentioned. They can be identified, if you don't notice it right when they're born, by their lips and fingernails getting blue every now and then and by their being "pited." (potted?) They never live very long. One mother's "blue baby" lived for seven months and was the "smartest" baby she ever had. The baby never cried, but just sat still and looked at pictures in books. Then one night she took pneumonia and died right off. The doctors were puzzled as to why she died until the mother told them she had been a "blue baby." The doctor who had brought her did not recall this, but the mother reminded him that it was at night and their kerosene lamp was very dim and he might not have noticed. A neighbor whose baby was born about the time this one died heard someone say she was afraid this was a blue baby, too. She got to studying and worrying over it, and didn't go to sleep night or day for a whole month until she lost her mind. She had been thirty when she married and was extremely desirous of having a child. The thought that it might be a "blue baby" and die some day drove her insane.

The sanitary facilities for childbirth in the home are woefully inadequate. Preparation consists of collecting old cloths for pads and navel dressings, of getting ready clean sheets and rubber sheeting in some homes, but in others, old, dirty quilts that can be thrown away. A mother's ideas of sanitation were revealed in her telling of a dream she had had the night before. In the dream she suddenly realized that her sister was about to give birth to a baby on the new $12.75 mattress which is the pride of her life—she has never even let the baby wet it. She loves her sister, but she could not see her mattress ruined. She ran quickly and found some old, torn quilts she was saving for rags, put them on a cot and made her sister get on it. "You can have your baby here," she told her sister, "but not on my fine mattress and clean sheets!" When instrumental deliveries have to be made, the kitchen table is called into service. Hot water is usually available and one or two mothers said they had Lysol, but any other antiseptics or germicides have to be brought by the doctor. Kidney and blood poison, convulsions, milk leg, and other serious conditions were reported as having developed and having been treated at home. One mother had "the child bed fever" twice when "grannies" were attending her and finally had to have doctors called in both times. This one is insisting that her pregnant married daughter go to a hospital to be confined since she knows the husband can afford it and knows from her own sad experience that it is the best thing to do. Two who have been to hospitals for childbirth recommend them highly for the rest and waiting on one gets; two others condemn hospital care because of neglect and ill treatment.

Miscarriages, being unexpected, find the mother even less well prepared and the doctor longer in coming. One mother lay alone bleeding all day long last spring while her husband went ten miles to town to try to find a doctor who would come out. It was much worse than having a baby, she thought. Another told of "passing it" while walking home from the field one "evening." She had on overalls and so no one saw. Because it was the busy season she went back to work the next day without having any medical attention. She feels that she's never been the same inside since. Another has had two miscarriages since her second marriage and only a "granny" to come in after both of them. They were "awful bad" and this is the mother who is sparing herself all she can during a current pregnancy to avoid another. Yet her washerwoman is a "granny" who has to be away so much that the mother is still doing washing some weeks since her husband *has* to have his overalls.

Attitudes toward childbearing are the core of interest in the study of fertility, for it is the psychological reaction to external factors, such as traditional and economic pressures, which finally translates these societal forces into effects on the birth rate. These attitudes are difficult to state summarily. Undoubtedly there is ambivalence. The traditional pattern of the glory and the actual or imagined value of a large number of children pull in one direction, while the desire to avoid the suffering of childbearing, the trouble of caring for another child, and the responsibility of another mouth to be fed and body to be clothed pull in the other. An approximate balance of these forces means that the former wins out because children keep arriving when a laissez-faire policy is adopted. And yet the trend, indicated by the verbal expressions of the mothers on the subject and confirmed by quantitative birth rate data is an increase in the response to the latter forces accompanied by a greater availability of techniques for preventing births.

The ambivalence is manifested almost universally among these mothers in the difference in attitudes toward past and future childbearing. There is pride in having borne the number they have, yet almost never is there expressed a desire for more. The most common example of the first is the ever present suggestion of self-esteem in both words and intonation of answers to the question of how many children the mother of a large family has—"Eleven. I done my share, didn't I?" or "Ten and all a-living." The pride becomes even more exaggerated when the larger sized families of the previous generation are being reported—"My mammy raised and married thirteen," "I was one of seventeen," or, and this was the largest number reported and that by a husband glowing with vicarious elation over the achievement, "I was next to the youngest of twenty-two." The bearing, "raising," and "marrying off" of children are everywhere recognized as being a positive achievement, a contribution to the world as well as to the immediate family. The remembrance of qualms or regrets over discovering one's self pregnant fades with time as does the pain of childbirth, leaving the note of pride prevailing with regard to the past.

On the other hand, every one of the mothers with babies of two or under, either explicitly or by inference, expressed the attitude, "I hope this is the last one." So many of them used these identical words, that the stereotyped expression may be interpreted as the verbalization of a fairly rigid and universal attitude, although in most cases the effecting of the wish was limited to "hoping." There are variations from this modal attitude, of course, although so few in the direction of wanting more children that they can all be cited. A woman who had a hysterectomy fifteen years ago after her second child would "give her life" to have another baby. Another, who is still in bed from the same operation following her twelfth child, moans bitterly that she can't have any more children. Less marked modifications are shown in the statement of one whose baby is now six, "I guess four's enough to feed and clothe; but now since they're all at school, I think sometimes I sure would like to have a little 'un around the house. I guess I'd want one if it wasn't for the nine months." Another's answer to how she felt when she knew a seventh child was coming after she hadn't had one in seven years was, "I was glad—I guess we all like little 'uns. I 'spect you'd like to have a little 'un yourself after all these years, wouldn't you?"

Deviations from the modal attitudes are more frequent in the direction of actively not wanting children than in the direction of wanting them. All the resentment against having borne twelve unwanted babies was summed up in a mother's bitter wish that she could have had just one child before marrying so that she would have known what it meant and, therefore, not have married. A widow who had six children in eight years, although attracted by men, swears that she will not marry again until she is fifty and knows she will have no more. The knowledge of each new pregnancy often results in a period of inner rebellion before there is an acceptance of the inevitable. A mother, who had been cheerful, cordial, and expansive, offered a sullen greeting on a later visit, "Look at the mess I've got myself into since you was here last." Many told of crying for days when "I found I was that way again." Attitudes of other people toward the mothers concerning their pregnancy and childbearing correspond fairly closely with their own inner feelings. At first there is usually pity and often reproach or scorn about "getting caught" but this gradually changes to commendation and congratulations at birth. One woman was always ashamed to go visit her mother after she had "missed" a month for she knew her condition was the first thing she would be asked about and she dreaded the scolding which being pregnant always brought. And yet her mother boasted of her own numerous children and especially of her forty-three living grandchildren and attached great importance to big families.

The modal attitude of not wanting children is not accompanied by a modal practice of preventing them. Certain difficulties inhered in the securing of information on contraceptive practices. In the first place lack of privacy in the interviews prevented discussion of such matters with some mothers. Then, the impossibility of using technical terms because of the mothers' ignorance, or of using "vulgar, menfolks' words" for fear of offending them made for a lack of concreteness and specificity when contraception or sexual relations were discussed. In spite of the hindrance imposed by this lack of a vocabulary, there was almost always a willingness to talk about such matters even though circumlocution made the process of conveying information cumbersome. Of the sixty-nine mothers questioned as to the use of contraceptives, only eight replied in the affirmative. Three use condoms, two douches, one diaphragm and jelly, and two practice withdrawal. Although every effort was made to clarify the question so the mother would understand she was being asked about contraception and not about induced abortions, it is possible that this may not have been understood by all and that a few negative replies should have been affirmative. It is even more probable that to some of them the words, "birth control," do not include withdrawal and that some of those who answered "no" actually do practice this method. An illustration of the euphemistic phraseology employed occurred when one mother tried to explain that this was the method she and her husband used. Her answer was metaphorical: "Well, I always say that when you chew tobacco, it don't make so much mess if you spit it out the window." Another described the same method in the words of advice which had been given her by an older woman, "If you don't want butter, pull the dasher out in time!"

In spite of confusion and misunderstanding of terms, it is undoubtedly true that the modal practice in this group is to use no contraceptive methods whatsoever. Yet of forty-two who expressed opinions, thirty-seven declared themselves in favor of birth control. In these favorable opinions there are many evidences of a fairly recent change in point of view as well as vestiges of former attitudes. The most common comment was, "I think it's a bigger sin to have children you can't provide for (or "haven't the strength to take care of,") than to do something to keep from having them." The range of attitudes extended to a few who completely disapproved on religious grounds and bolstered their views with statements such as, "The Lord causes what he wishes," or a less theological statement of the same fatalism, "I believe you will have as many as you're supposed to." Next to these were several who believed birth control injurious to health and one who gave no reason for disapproval except a eulogy on her love for her children.

Those who approved often felt the necessity for rationalizing their approval on the basis of health or the welfare of unborn or already-born children. One showed keen insight into psychological matters by explaining how being unwanted affected adversely the personality development of a child. Older women sometimes made semifacetious comments. One after hearing that the visitor had only one child said knowingly, "H'mm—you're smart, ain't ye?" and another, "They've got right smart along that line nowadays." Other more serious older women who never used contraceptives themselves said they had advised their married daughters to do so. Only one woman reported perfect success in the practice of contraception over a period of years. All of the other users were less enthusiastic over contraception since they had all had failures. One woman told how her mother scrimped and saved $10 to buy her a very special sort of "serene" (syringe) which did no good at all. Most have heard that there are effective methods now, but they do not know what they are nor where to go to get reliable information about them.

As a group they are rather disillusioned about doctors. A common complaint is that "doctors tell you not to have any more children but won't tell you nothing to do about it." Some have very vague ideas about contraceptive devices and their cost; one woman mentioned that the things they advertise in magazines to keep you from having babies cost more than having a baby would. Fourteen mothers asked directly "what to do," and some were told of the newly-established contraceptive service of their county health units. One of these mothers, revisited some months later, was so delighted over at last having the fear of pregnancy removed that she could scarcely talk of anything else.

Because childbearing and its prevention are of such great significance for students of population, we recapitulate to the extent of attempting a composite, modal description of attitudes and practices relating to childbearing and contraception. The mother is proud of having borne the children she has although she may not have wished for another before she became pregnant each time. This pride appears to have its basis in several sources: the extension of self in the producing of a big family—probably more important here than in higher economic classes as compensation for lack of other tangible possessions; the furnishing of evidence of the woman's fertility and her husband's virility, and of her husband's manifestation of affection and sexual desire for herself; the sense of virtue resulting from having provided field workers of economic value to her own family linked with a vague notion of having done something constructive for humanity at large. On the other hand, because of a realization of the physiological burden, the work of bringing up children, and the knowledge that they mean expense, the mother, in spite of a conditioned fondness for babies, definitely and positively does not wish for more children. And yet, although she has heard of the existence of contraceptive devices—chiefly as something used by the wilder courting couples and obtained from filling stations—she does not practice contraception for various reasons, but simply hopes that another baby will not be her lot.

An estimate of the relative importance of the various reasons for not practicing contraception is indicated in the following order of their listing:

1. Inertia in changing established habits—the modal aged thirty-nine-year-old mother has probably learned of contraception since the establishment of a routine of sexual relations with her husband;

2. Insufficient knowledge of contraceptive methods, the effective devices, where they can be obtained, and too much embarrassment over a taboo subject to seek intelligently for such knowledge—this augmented by her physician's practice of giving no contraceptive information even when health needs indicate it;

3. The expense factor, which alone would be sufficient to keep at least half of the families from using contraception, for they simply have no cash to be spent for what must be at first an experimental venture;

4. The lack of willingness and cooperation on the part of the husband, which may be due to any of the reasons listed for the wife, or to the fact that he does not have to do the bearing of or caring for the children and hence is less concerned over there being more;

5. Religious prejudice.

It is on the second point that direct attacks can be made by birth control propagandists and eugenists. The first, fourth, and fifth can be removed only gradually by increasing motivation to share the advantages of small families through education, enlightenment, and the presence of economic opportunity to climb. The third and very often the determining reason can be removed only by establishing clinics which provide service free or at nominal cost, as do the public health contraceptive centers, or by revamping the whole economic system so that farm tenants may get a larger income. The rational argument that birth control costs less than having babies does not hold where contraceptive supplies must be paid for in cash while doctors and midwives still bring babies on credit.

Thus the major problems of regional and occupational overpopulation and the bankruptcy of cash crop agriculture intertwine and come to a focus in the life of the tenant farm mother. A mother's farewell epitomized her situation and attitudes: "You can tell 'em you saw a woman with thirteen children still going strong and doing more work than *any* town woman—but I hope you don't find me with another when you come back."

Chapter 10

Of Child "Raising"

THE PRIMARY interest in the mothers as producers naturally extends to the children as products. Moreover, the increasing emphasis on the environmental determiners of quality is elevating the "raising" function of mothers to a level of importance equal to that of the "bearing" function. If efficiency in the first accompanied prolificness in the second, much of the alarm created by eugenists over differential birth rates would be dispelled.

Rearing, or "raising" in Southern tenant farm language, in its broadest sense includes whatever is transmitted to a child by his parents from birth to maturity. In content it may be analyzed into three parts: (1) the supplying of physical needs—food, shelter, clothing, medical treatment; (2) the emotional conditioning and the translation of the general cultural heritage into assimilable doses ranging from simple habit formation and language acquisition to morals, religion, and political views; (3) the affording of opportunities for extra-home experience such as schooling, library facilities, parties, and movies. (The parent is not wholly responsible for this part since it is also affected by geographical location and other external factors.) The process of emotional and intellectual development taking place in the child through the constant interplay of personalities is generally referred to in common parlance as something impressed from above by the parent and is termed training, rearing or raising. We shall consider the aspects of raising in the order listed above, and, while no measures of efficiency are attempted, we point to certain excellences and deficiencies in the several phases.

The supplying of some of the physical needs has already been described. In the matter of diet it is hard to know where parental responsibility begins, for one runs into the larger question of an individual's responsibility for economic status and for his own knowledge and training. The effects as observed run all the way from obvious deficiencies, as in the case of the emaciated boy who had lived through both pellagra and rickets, to the finest appearing physical specimens one could find anywhere, as in the case of a family of eight healthy and handsome children. Whether calorie, mineral, and vitamin needs are met can be determined only by careful biochemical studies. All we can say here is that except in years of extraordinary hardship the mothers do cook three meals a day, although few of these would meet the modern urban standards for a balanced meal; that most of the children have milk, some fresh vegetables from gardens in summer, and a limited amount of canned ones in winter; that they eat a great deal of hot bread, sweet potatoes, syrup, and salt pork; and that in the poorer half of the families the variety of food is quite limited.

As for shelter, there is probably little actual damage to health from the substandard housing except for drafts and insufficient heating, which are predisposing conditions to respiratory diseases, and for inadequate screens and toilet facilities, which may cause typhoid or other diseases of the intestinal tract. Crowding cannot be measured by the same persons-per-room ratio as in city slums because the problem of ventilation and fresh air scarcely enters. Moreover, the social and psychological effects of crowding are less serious than in cities because of the abundance of outdoors available except in midwinter. Similarly, in the matter of clothing there is probably no injury to health except in a few cases where there may be an actual lack of enough warm garments for adequate protection during the coldest months. Here, however, the social and psychological effects of poor and shabby clothing are greater. The children who go to rural consolidated schools are thrown into groups including children of owners, and comparisons and contrasts of clothes are inevitable. Some tenant children are transported into towns, where the contrasts are even greater. Clothes probably play a great part in forming town children's stereotype of the "bus" or country children as "dumb."

In lack of medical treatment there is more actual detriment to health than in any other of the physical aspects save possibly diet. The modal pattern is dosing with Black Draught or castor oil for any attack of anything until it becomes very serious. These two home remedies were mentioned more often than all others combined. In home treatment the mother's ignorance of biology, hygiene, and elementary nursing is the chief defect, for tenant children do not usually suffer from lack of attention when they are ill. Examples follow to illustrate the sort of health care for which ignorance or superstition is to blame. One two-year-old baby, flushed with a fever, was given an all-day sucker because, "he's kinda sick." A mother who subscribes to several magazines and seems rather superior in general background told how she cured her baby's hand of a bad burn which had festered. She thought she had seen the "receipt" in one of the farm papers, but she was not certain. At any rate, she took some fresh cow manure, tied it in a little sack of cheesecloth, boiled it, and to the "tea" added a tablespoonful of hog lard. She cooled this essence, applied it to the burn, wrapped around the hand a cloth soaked in it, and in three days the burn was completely cured without a scar. Another mother had cured rheumatism by drinking cocklebur tea twice a day. Another gives her children garlic as worm medicine, while another claims garlic is good to reduce high blood pressure. Two older women deplore the fact that doctors will no longer let blood to keep down blood pressure and one told of a neighbor completely cured of "high blood" by losing great quantities of blood when a cow "hooked" her.

Although some mantels were seen which were loaded with patent medicines or occasionally prescriptions, the usual household has few standard medicaments. "Dew-sores" were almost epidemic during September and were either neglected or treated with whatever sort of salve that happened to be around the house. A little later in the season a number of children had heels blistered from badly fitted, cheap, new shoes; three of these had become infected and the most serious one was being treated with only turpentine. If such local infections are survived, their after effects are not usually serious. More important is the neglect of chronic troubles from lack of money for medical treatment, or from inadequate or "quack" treatment. One mother can't pay to have "this here cross-eyed knee-baby's eyes straightened," although he has failed in school for two years and the teacher says it is mainly because he cannot see. In many of the children tonsils and adenoids were suspected from facial expression and tone of voice, and need of dental attention was quite obvious. A crippled son can stay in the hospital only so long as the money collected by the church lasts; then he has to come home and wait for more to be collected before he gets additional treatment. At the other end of the scale is a family who have kept their two children continually under the care of the best city specialists although they have been criticized by neighbors for spending so much on doctors. Their children at sixteen and seventeen are now in excellent health, although ten years ago they feared a certain chronic and severe bronchial trouble in the daughter was incurable.

Observation and accounts of the mothers themselves indicate that the chief reason for lack of medical treatment is economic. Case after case was reported where treatment for one thing or another had been stopped because there was no money to pay for it any longer. One of these was a woman with "eating cancer," which had been much improved as long as she could continue electric treatments; another with pellagra is supposed to have a certain number of dollar and five-dollar "shots" every spring, but hasn't been able to afford them for two years. Often there had been a diagnosis that an operation was needed, but unless the family was already under the care of the public welfare department, the tenants often either did not know how to go about getting free medical aid or they did not wish to apply for "charity." Some doctors continue to answer calls when patients do not pay; others do not. The burden of medical expense seems very heavy to tenants and the item which is offered as unquestioned evidence of a good year is, "We even paid our doctor bill."

Another reason given for inadequacy of medical treatment is that some doctors, perhaps suspicious of getting no remuneration, perhaps irritated at the inconvenience of driving a long way out in the country, perhaps because they consider tenants as hardly people—just a degree or so removed from "niggers"—do not give the same quality of service to tenants which they give to other patients. Some of the reports of such instances were, no doubt, distorted intentionally or by ignorance, but they are indicative of the situation. A doctor who did not come back to see a sick child until too late told the mother it had died of "purple-itis," a very rare disease, which he could not have cured anyway. Another doctor swore at a mother who went to him because of acute suffering during pregnancy, "My God, I didn't get you that way and I can't do anything for it!" Several weeks later another doctor found a serious condition of the uterus, which yielded to correct treatment so that all pain was relieved and a normal delivery of the baby was possible. A child with pellagra was treated for eczema

Documenting a Region

In the year *Mothers of the South* was published, Margaret Hagood and her colleague Harriet Herring experimented with another kind of documentary, a comprehensive photographic study of life in thirteen counties of piedmont North Carolina, the same counties in which she had conducted interviews for the book.

It was a bold conception. Herring envisioned a series of photographs of the land that would range from the panoramic to the highly detailed, that would convey a sense of what it was like to live in the piedmont and yet would illustrate such things as the difference between good and bad soil, good and bad plowing, the effects of erosion, terracing, and the like. She wanted pictures to show the development of each crop from sowing to harvest, animals from razorback hogs wandering half wild in the woods to pedigreed bulls, fit, as she put it, for "portraits." She wanted to record on film the processes of farm life, folkways, people. To round out the study she also wanted detailed photographs of manufacturing processes, company towns, factories, and mill workers.

In Washington, Roy Stryker and his gifted staff at the Historical Section of the Farm Security Administration were breaking new ground in documentary photography. Their purposes were close to those of Hagood and Herring, and Stryker agreed to a cooperative experiment. He assigned

Dorothea Lange and Marion Post to the project and the four women joined forces.[1]

In the spring, summer, and fall of 1939 they traveled the North Carolina countryside, Lange and Post taking pictures, Hagood and Herring taking careful notes. The result was a collection of revealing photographs and an evocative and informative set of accompanying notes. Over a hundred of the pictures were publicly exhibited at the University of North Carolina in the spring of 1940.

The following photographs are chosen from hundreds which have survived from the project. They provide a visual context for *Mothers of the South*. Together with the accompanying notes, here excerpted, they show once again how intent Hagood and her colleagues were on finding new ways to show the south as they perceived it.

Photographs and excerpts from the notes are printed here with the kind permission of the Southern Historical Collection of the University of North Carolina.

1. See Roy Stryker and Nancy Wood, *In This Proud Land* (Greenwich, Conn.: New York Graphic Society, 1973), for Stryker's own evaluation of the work of the Historical Section of the Farm Security Administration, which produced 270,000 photographs under his leadership. See also William Scott, *Documentary Expression and Thirties America* (New York: Oxford University Press, 1973), pp. 11, 14, 29.

These pictures were taken at the home of a tenant farmer living near Hurdle Mills, North Carolina. The mother of the family was thirty-three years old, had been married at twenty-one, and had four children ranging from six months to nine years. Both parents were raised on farms and had been sharecroppers all their lives.

The woman in a sunbonnet, wearing knitted mitts to protect her hands, was photographed at the annual cleanup day of a Primitive Baptist church near Gordonton, North Carolina. She was called "Queen."

Here are two examples of tenant houses: the first, a log house with a clapboard addition, was inhabited by a Negro sharecropper. The second was the home of a white tenant.

Margaret Hagood and Marion Post attended a cornshucking on a farm near Stem, North Carolina. These are three of the pictures they took that day: *(below)* the shucking; *(on the facing page)* the meal being served, and the women washing the dishes. Hagood's notes read in part: "This was an all-day cornshucking with about 20 men working at one time, although some of the morning workers were replaced by others in the afternoon. The food was prepared by the wife and her four sisters-in-law and one Negro woman.... Two tables were put together in the dining room. All the white men ate first, then the table was cleared and dishes washed and the table re-set for the white women and children. After they ate the dishes were washed and the table reset again for the Negro men."

The family group eating watermelon lived about six miles north of Roxboro, North Carolina. The house is log with a frame addition.

A husband and wife have taken their tobacco to Durham, North Carolina, to sell it. Here they sit on the tobacco as they try to decide whether to accept the price offered.

and lost almost all the flesh from one leg before the doctor finally changed his diagnosis. In giving descriptions of their own health, mothers often quote (or misquote) the doctor as saying the trouble is just a "nervous heart" or other equally vague appellations. Several who had been diagnosed as having "high blood" or "low blood" had received no suggestion of diet modifications.

As deplorable as the lack of medical treatment is the pseudo-treatment by a "quack." In a neighborhood characterized by a high proportion of illiteracy, a certain doctor, already referred to, has a great many patients. He is a licensed M.D. but has been outlawed by his professional colleagues in the city and is not permitted to bring his patients to any of the hospitals there. He sets himself up as a pellagra specialist, but his treatment of this disease is reputed to be dosage with a weak solution of hydrochloric acid. He knows how to talk to country people and has convinced many of them that the doctors at the hospital use clinic patients to experiment on and have often killed them.

There was an opportunity to see first hand and in actual operation the technique by which another sort of exploitation of ignorance is carried out. During a visit in a striphouse with a mother, father, and three or four children, a well-dressed, middle-aged woman drove up in an automobile. The father went outside to speak to her and a part of the conversation between them was overheard, "My old lady's got the rheumatism right bad; why don't you come in?" To this the mother commented, "What's he asking her in for? He knows I done spent all the money I got off my patch yesterday and can't buy no medicine." The agent accepted the invitation and climbed the ladder clumsily with her jars and bottles. Inside she refused a chair saying she could talk better standing and she didn't want anyone to leave because she probably had just what everyone needed for whatever ailments he might have.

She proceeded to give a discourse upon each of the three medicines she was selling. No. 1 was a salve which would not only cure any local infection such as toe-itch, ring worm, eczema, impetigo, pimples, dew-sores, risings, boils, and carbuncles, but if the trouble was caused from something inside—bad blood or poisons being generated—it would draw out through the sore all the cause of it so that the sore would never come back. Furthermore, the salve positively cured piles, dandruff, and blackheads, and could also be used for "doo-itches" (douches). No. 2 was a tooth powder which, if used in time, would prevent pyorrhea, or if used after the onset of the disease would cure it completely and tighten the teeth back up in their sockets. Its advantages over all other sorts of dentifrices lay in its remarkable germ killing powers, which were so lasting that if one used it twice a day, it completely prevented him from catching any sort of disease in which the germ entered through the mouth—you don't have to bother with vaccinations, inoculations, or other preventive measures.

The first two, she admitted, are really only ordinary medicines. The third, called Vi-Ava, is the most wonderful discovery in the history of medicine, a substance invented by a doctor in California which actually regenerates nerve tissue. Since the nerves control the body, any ailment can be cured by putting in order the nerves which control that particular part of the body affected. Of course, if it is just a minor trouble, it is more sensible to treat it with No. 1 or No. 2 because, "there's one thing you can say about Vi-Ava—it *is* expensive, although of course it's worth ten times the price if you have a serious ailment." Vi-Ava cures *any*thing and for this reason doctors will not recommend it because they know they will lose their patients if they tell them of this wonderful cure and doctors cannot make a living unless there are sick people. Vi-Ava is put up in eight different forms, each appropriate for a special part of the body. It is so precious that the sample case with minute amounts of each costs $7.50. There is Form A for all the nerves, Form B for the blood, C for the kidneys, D for the stomach, E for the liver, F for the intestines—a laxative, G for infections, and H for the "organs—you know." For her rheumatism the mother should use Form B, which will work on the nerves that control the blood stream and force it to remove all those poisons stored up in the joints as well as keep any more from forming.

Interspersed with this factual information were all sorts of sympathy, attention, and confidence-getting stories. The agent was a widow who had been left all alone in the world with three children to support. She herself had rheumatism so badly that she could hardly walk and Vi-Ava had completely cured it. She is very charitable and illustrated this by a story of an old man who had not been able to go out of the house for twenty years. He was once a wealthy farmer but had lost all his land and money paying doctors for unsuccessful treatments when she found him in a dirty mill town. She felt so sorry for him that she persuaded his doctor to let her take over the case. She treated him free with Vi-Ava and had him out on the streets in two weeks.

She held the group spellbound—almost in tears over the sad condition of people before they found Vi-Ava and elated when they were made whole again. She inspected each member of the family for apparent ills and diagnosed and prescribed one of her medicines for each of them. The only note of humor introduced into the situation was when she prescribed No. 1 to cure the breaking out on the baby's face, which turned out to be candy someone had given him the day before. The children laughed over her mistake, but she was not stopped by a minor slip and in a few minutes had the rapt attention of all over the story of when her son was in an accident and lost quarts of blood. He was told that he couldn't live but Vi-Ava, Form B, quickly had him well again. After nearly an hour she got down to business and, when she found the family had no money left from their yesterday's tobacco sales, she departed quickly.

All were deeply affected by her oratory and sat quietly for several minutes. The illiterate mother finally sighed and broke the silence with a shrewd observation, "My! Can't she talk, though! I guess I'd 'a bought some if I'd 'a had the money. But—I guess I ought not to say this because I don't know nothing about such things (this almost in apology to the visitor for speaking critically of another "outside" person)—I feel about it just like my mammy used to say when she'd look at a bottle of medicine—she could read—and see all the things listed it was supposed to be good for, that she couldn't put much faith in it curing the one thing that was the matter with her." However, the agent's clothes and car testified that she had found other clients not so skeptical.

In the second general aspect of raising we come to the part of the broader definition ordinarily denoted by the term. We shall treat this part somewhat chronologically. The baby begins his life as the most adored, petted, and cherished member of the family and usually continues in this rôle until he is displaced by a younger brother or sister. Seven-eighths of the mothers said they spoiled their babies. Variations from the modal pattern of a moderate degree of spoiling are more frequent in the direction of spoiling to excess than in the direction of no spoiling. A common explanation of favoritism toward a child is that he has been the baby twice, that is, that the baby born next after him had died. Older children arriving from school often run to pick up and pet the baby. Husky fathers are excused for demonstration of affection toward the baby—in one case with the remark that the father was from a big family and had always been used to having a baby around. Several times the fact that a child had been the "baby" for more than two or three years was offered as justification for his being still spoiled at a later age. A shift in sex in the sequence of children makes for extra devotion as in cases where girls were born after several consecutive boys.

In tenant homes there is little familiarity with modern rules for the care and feeding of infants. Only five mothers had ever nursed any of their babies on a "schedule" and the notion was new to some and incomprehensible to a few. A baby is nursed when he cries and usually for as long as he wishes. He is considered "smart" if he doesn't cry for "ninny" often, yet there seems to be little training directed toward this. One mother boasted that her baby was so smart that once when she went to help cook at a cornshucking, he lay on a bed for nearly three hours without crying. This feat attracted attention and finally, some of the older women got after her and said, "You take that baby right up and feed it. You don't have to starve him to death just because he's smart." Seventeen months is the arithmetic mean of the weaning ages reported, but the figure is possibly misleading since it combines a group of weaning ages from nine to fifteen months, where weaning was necessitated by another pregnancy, with a group of much older ages, which are more common if another pregnancy does not occur. The baby is rarely weaned early and, as he gets older, he makes his wants known with words. A mother was literally forced by a two-year-old daughter to nurse her three or four times during an hour's visit, although the mother protested that she believed "when they get old enough to call for ninny, they are old enough to do without it." Another child of four who kept pulling at his mother's breast was scolded and shamed, but finally allowed to nurse.

There is little special preparation of food to supplement the mother's milk, although quite a few babies were being fed plain or diluted cow's milk in bottles because their mothers' milk had failed. One of these was a thirteenth child and the mother says that if she had known how much more freedom it gives her to be able to leave a baby for more than an hour at a time, she would have used bottles with her others. She continues, however, to nurse the baby to get it to sleep, since only one of her breasts is diseased. This is the most common technique of getting the baby to sleep and he is eased onto a bed afterwards. Some of the babies are rocked to sleep either in their mothers' arms or in old-fashioned cradles with rockers. Others will not go to sleep unless the mother or a brother or sister lies down on the bed with them. Only two of the mothers put their babies down and leave them alone to go to sleep regardless of whether they cry or not. Naps are sometimes as regular as one in the morning and one in the "evening," but there is little adherence to or insistence upon routine.

In terms of conventional standards of habit formation an evaluation of the infant's raising is low. There is irregularity of feeding and sleeping hours and delay in teaching control of the bladder. There is a widely followed formula for the latter which does not require much time or trouble on the part of the mother. She waits until the first summer after the baby has learned to walk and then lets him stay outdoors in the yard without any diaper or pants on. It is claimed that he will become accustomed to urinating without wetting his clothes and when he is clad again in pants the next winter, he will make it known when he wants to "pee" so as not to ruin them.

In terms of emotional development, the infant's training has certain aspects of positive value. He is certainly "wanted" and is treated as if he were. There may be too much giving in to his wishes, too much attention, but the early assurance of affection is recognized to afford one of the greatest assets against all sorts of strain and conflict in later personality development. Moreover, there is an absence of the continual struggle and conflict which often accompanies the forcing of an infant to an arbitrary routine and this period of life appears to be fairly free from frustration.

A surprising sequel is that, after two or three years of being the center of the family's affection, the "baby" is not more resentful about becoming graduated to the stage of "knee-baby" when the next child appears upon the scene. A few cases of temporary jealousy were reported, but only one case was observed where the experience seemed to be of a serious traumatic nature. The modal pattern is for the knee-baby to join quickly with the rest of the family in adoration of the youngest. In two instances the knee-babies seemed to regard the babies as their especial property and care, since they were more closely associated with the mother and her new child than were other members of the family. When one mother came home from the hospital with a new baby, the knee-baby pulled a chair up by the side of the bed and sat there almost steadily during the week the mother stayed in bed. After she got up, he considered it his duty or privilege to sit in the same spot whenever the baby was napping and he feels proprietary rights because of this sentinel duty. Another knee-baby of four is inordinately proud that she can carry her younger brother. On one visit a knee-baby of seven was found taking care of her own baby sister and her little niece while her mother picked cotton. She was very devoted and attentive to them and showed them off to the visitor with great pride.

The exceptional case was where the knee-baby reacted to his displacement from the favored position as might be expected.

A scene from a visit illustrates this and also the mother's complete lack of understanding of the situation. When the mother took up her six-months-old baby from a pallet on the kitchen floor to change it, the knee-baby promptly seized the opportunity to arrange himself comfortably on the quilt and pillows. When the mother was through with the changing and told him to move, he screamed, "No, *I* want to be the baby!" She insisted that he move and he refused for several minutes, whereupon she reached to the top of the safe for a long switch, said, "Well, you're *not* the baby now, so you can be whipped," and proceeded to switch him with one arm while she held the baby with the other. He still refused to budge in spite of the whipping. Finally, she reached down and dragged him off the pallet onto the floor where he lay crying for the rest of the visit, occasionally interrupting his sobs to reach over and pinch the baby, which had again been placed on the pallet.

This incident may serve also to introduce the whole matter of discipline and "making children mind." Subjection of the child's will to parental authority is still a firmly-held ideal, although modifications are becoming necessary. Whipping or whupping (pronounced who͝oping) is the rule. "You just can't raise children without whupping 'em," is a very generally accepted maxim, although disciplinary patterns vary greatly. In one family the parents have never touched one of their children, nor were they themselves whipped in their own upbringing, and yet the children mind and work "a heap better than them that's beat to death," reports their mother. At the other extreme, an old woman thinks this way of raising children without whipping is "raising 'em for the gallows." Even she, however, does not believe in whipping them before they are a month old, as her daughter does. She says she just can't believe that a baby three weeks old understands what the whipping's for—she never started whipping her own until they were two or three months old.

In seven-eighths of the families the mother has the burden of the discipline and in the other eighth, either the father or both parents. The usual description of the situation, stated explicitly in about one-third of the cases, is that the mother whips most, but that the children mind their father best. This is often explained by the fact that, "they're with me more," or "they're used to me," or "they don't see so much of him." The pattern of the mother whipping most is also accompanied by characterization of the father such as, "He just goes on like nothing was happening and pretends not to see when they need it," "I have to whip because he's too easy going," or "He won't whip because he's too crazy about them." Yet in some of the families, "whichever one ain't busiest whips," or "I whip 'em if they need it in the house and he does if they have to have it in the field." One father is proud of the way he can make his nine children mind. When he was paralyzed, they thought at first they could get away with meanness, but he would have some of the older children bring the offending one to his bed for a whipping with his unparalyzed arm. In one family a sister who mothers four younger brothers and sisters has to do all the whipping, and in many families where older sisters have charge of younger children at times, they whip them because otherwise they couldn't manage them.

Whipping is not the only disciplinary technique employed. A mother and a grandmother both constantly threatened a three-year-old girl with a "Big Black Nig," to keep her from doing things she shouldn't. Another admitted she was the sort who would say, "If you do such and such a thing, I'll whip you," and then not keep her word—but it worked sometimes. One dwelt at length on the individual differences of her children, which necessitate different treatments. She whips most of them every day, but her eight-year-old daughter has always been so smart that she's never had but one whipping. Another also told of one child that she was able to manage only by "talking to," while she could always just whip the others and get it over with. Several designated "talking to" as a device supplementary to whipping. A young mother set forth rather advanced ideas when her five-year-old boy fell and bumped his head without crying. She explained that she had never picked him up or petted him after a hurt, in order to train him not to cry. In another family which doesn't believe in whipping, the father is always "wrastling" with the boys. The mother says they frolic and carry on so that sometimes she has to take a stick of stovewood to the whole bunch of them. A religious woman never whipped her daughter, but just explained to her what Jesus would want her to do and, according to the mother, she did it. No examples of rewards or deprivations as disciplinary techniques were observed or reported except the payment for certain tasks. It may well be that their level of living does not permit many luxuries from which a child might be deprived, or for which he might be motivated to good conduct.

According to the mothers, most of the whipping is for the children's fighting or fussing with each other. "You know how a big family is—always fussing." Next in frequency of reported causes is their "not minding," especially their keeping on doing something they have been told to stop, or not coming home when they have been told to. Only a few reported having to whip children to make them work.

Training in work is a phase of raising which is far more important on the tenant farm than in the urban home. Parents are generally proud of the early achievements of their children. The story of daughters who started making bread when they were so little that they had to stand on a chair to reach the bread tray on the table was heard so often that it was recognized to be a stereotyped boast. Many who had sons from ten to fourteen bragged that they could "plow like a man." The mean age at which the boys learned to plow is eleven and with a few exceptions after the age of fourteen this accomplishment is taken for granted.

The mothers were not able to be very specific about how they train children so young to work in the house and the field —it is simply taken for granted that children will work and they do. Several mothers think taking them to the field when they're babies will make them start early because they will want to do what they see their parents doing. Another mother explained thus the graduation of household tasks with age: "They can begin toting in wood a stick at a time when they're two. Soon after I start 'em to drying knives and forks, because they can't break them, and when they're a little older, the other dishes. They can sweep by six and carry water in small buckets and tend the baby. By ten they can clean house, make beds, and straighten up, and by twelve or thirteen can cook a meal if they have to." A unique exception in training children is that most girls are not taught to sew at home. This is due largely to the mother's not being willing to "trust them with my machine," which is often her most expensive and treasured possession.

What training the children get in financial responsibility usually comes in connection with "patches." None of the families gave their children regular allowances, but a sizable minority of the tobacco growing families let their children have, either separately or together, an acre or less of tobacco on which they do most of the work and from which they get the proceeds after the landowner's fourth or half is deducted. Some of the families who no longer do this said they had stopped it because it was too much trouble keeping the tobacco separated; instead, they give the children some money when the crop is sold. One mother brings her twelve-year-old daughter a present from town, "like a pair of socks," every time the daughter cleans up the whole house on Saturday morning while the mother goes into town to sell produce at the curb market. More generally, whatever money the children get comes in a lump sum in the fall and, like their parents, they are without cash during most of the year. One father does not give his boys all their crop money at once, but saves some for spring when they will be needing to buy clothes again. Another advances the children some of what he borrows on the crop during the summer and they pay it back out of their patch money in the fall. The bulk of this money is spent for clothing under the mother's supervision up to a certain age, and then at the discretion of the child. This age varies: a seventeen-year-old daughter will not buy even a pair of shoes unless her mother or older sister is with her; three boys of twelve, fourteen, and sixteen always want their mother to go with them to buy clothes, although she dislikes going to town intensely; but a nineteen-year-old girl figures out by herself everything she is going to spend and orders from Sears Roebuck or buys alone in town; another buys not only for herself, but for all her sisters since she makes all their clothes. One seventeen-year-old boy saved enough from his tobacco patch this year to go to a small junior college where the annual expense is only $200. This was the only instance reported of saving from patch money.

Accounts of spending for pleasure were only fragmentary. Two boys had bought bicycles from patch money, and a family of boys had purchased a truck. Children are sometimes given small amounts for fairs or circuses when these come in the fall and there is money on hand. One mother regretted never being able to give her children any money for candy since they are having to see the home supervisor of farm security about spending even for clothes this winter. The buying of pencils and paper for school work is often mentioned as a financial burden, but almost never in this or in the matter of spending money does there seem to be a budgeted or regularly planned arrangement. It is probable that the chief financial training which the tenant child gets to fit him for later life is practice in getting along without cash.

In the border-line area between those activities of the child which take place within the home and those extra-home ones which the parents control only to the extent of permitting the child to participate, is recreation, which, with age, shifts somewhat from the former to the latter category. Like other children, the preschool tenant child spends most of his time "playing," although from four or five years of age onwards, he has certain duties in housework and field work which begin to impinge upon his play time. By the time he is of school age, he is also old enough to be of some economic value and there is a more marked contrast between the amount of leisure time he has and that which an urban child enjoys. In summer he works in the field whenever there is work to be done for which he is suited. In all save rush periods, however, he, along with other members of the family, usually has Saturday afternoon and Sunday off. On these days there may be trips to town or visiting with his family at the homes of relatives or friends, where he can play with other children. It must be remembered, however, that he is not so lacking for companions near his own age as are children in smaller families, even when he stays right on "the place." With his brothers and sisters, sometimes with his father, or occasionally with close neighbors, there are opportunities to play, especially during the noon hour—when one family always "wrastle" and listen to the radio—and around supper time and immediately afterwards.

When school begins in September, free time is cut down.

The modal hour of getting up is five-thirty and there are plenty of chores to be done before leaving on the school bus, which may come by more than an hour before school begins. In some of the tobacco areas school "lets out" at noon for the first few weeks so that children may hasten home to help. All during the fall there is enough work to be done on the farm that the customary practice is to change to old clothes immediately on return from school and to work until supper time. After supper the period before bed time is ordinarily devoted to homework. During the winter, work slackens and afternoons may be more often used for recreation, but there are always the evening chores to be done. In spring farm work begins again.

One mother will not let her children go off to other people's houses even when they do not have to work because she knows the other mothers do not want lots of children around tearing up things. Then, too, she feels safer about her own children when they are at home, because children do all sorts of things when they are together and she fears they may break bones or get hurt. Another mother recognizes that her twelve-year-old boy does not get to play with other boys enough; they are afraid to come to her house on account of her feeble-minded child. And yet she will not let him go off "just to play" oftener than once a week because she does not feel it is right. She has had to whip him twice lately for slipping off to play. Sometimes the matter of class distinction enters; one mother does not want her children to associate with the children who live near because she thinks they are not the "right sort."

Policies become more sharply defined when the child reaches the courting age, especially if she is a girl. The modal practice is not to allow a daughter to go out anywhere with a boy unless the parents know and trust him. Even then she must go straight to some place and come straight back and "not go riding around over the country in automobiles at night."

Variations range from one mother's record that her daughter never left the house with a boy until she was married unless her father or brother was along, to the complete lack of supervision of one of the unmarried mothers, whose father is too old to manage even the younger children and whose mother is working in town in a sewing room and reputed to be "immoral." Several mothers spoke of their concern over their sons' chastity, but even these did not put nearly so stringent restrictions on the boys' going out.

The possibility of a girl's "getting in trouble" was almost always mentioned in connection with statements of policies about letting them go with boys. One mother will let her daughter have all the company she wants at home, but will not let her leave the house with a boy. Another lets her older daughter go out with her "steady" beau, but will not let her sixteen-year-old girl go anywhere except along with the older couple. Another has never allowed her seventeen- and nineteen-year-old daughters to use rouge or lipstick and she says her one hope and prayer is that she can "keep them straight." Only one mother wishes that her daughter would want to go to parties. She says she would be willing to let her go and to buy her dresses for them, but the daughter has not seemed to care about anything at all since her spell of sickness last spring. Mothers often explain their strictness on the basis of its being in keeping with the way they themselves were brought up. There is usually some degree of relaxation from their own upbringing, however, as several of the mothers were not allowed to have company even at home.

There seem to be several reasons for this strictness with daughters other than its being one manifestation of the general chronological lag in family patterns. Because of the lack of sophistication of the daughters, petting may lead more directly to sexual intercourse than in the case of urban girls. The same lack of knowledge of the ways of the modern world means that contraceptive devices are not so likely to be employed and that the result is more often pregnancy. It is probable also that a lack of recreational facilities and activities—in every neighborhood it was claimed that there are fewer parties now since the automobile—and a lack of common interests in sports, movies, and other subjects for conversation between a boy and a girl, make for difficulty in filling up the time of a date except with primary or secondary sex activities. Furthermore, as has been pointed out in connection with other matters, the fact that economic opportunity for climbing is so very slight leaves as the only way for the tenant to identify himself with the superior class, the clinging to the forms of middle class respectability. Since a daughter's going wrong is a heinous transgression against the mores and attaches stigma not only to the daughter herself, but also to the parents for not being the sort who "bring up their children right," and to the other brothers and sisters for not being "brought up right," there is small wonder that so many restrictions are placed upon the daughter's comings and goings and upon her associates. Judged from the context in which it occurs, the emphasis on not "getting into trouble," seems to be more tied up with the desire for social approval than with any morbid overemphasis on sex or with the strictly puritanical prevention of pleasure as has sometimes been alleged. Sex education of the daughters, which is given to daughters just before or at the time they begin to menstruate, is usually limited to meager information about menstruation and babies being born. From then on the weight of sex education is admonitions not to "get in trouble" with boys. Only one mother reported having given the same sort of instruction to her son as to her daughter. There was no investigation into what knowledge the father had imparted.

Of the extra-home influences, the school is undoubtedly the

most important in the training of the child. Since "Education" is often proposed as the slow but sure panacea of difficult socio-economic problems such as farm tenancy, we may well examine the attitudes and practices of tenant parents and children toward schooling. North Carolina has a law making school attendance compulsory between the ages of seven and fourteen and delegating the enforcement of attendance to the County Superintendent of Public Welfare. The Superintendent, however, has so many other duties that in only one of the counties visited was he enforcing the school attendance law with any rigidity.

The modal practice with regard to school attendance is to send the children to school fairly regularly unless there is some moderately urgent work to be done at home, in which case they are kept out. One extreme of divergence from this practice is in a family where a fifteen-year-old boy, bright looking and very attractive in appearance, has been kept out of school all his life until this year, or in another where only two of the eleven children have got as far as "stopping out in the fourth," and three of the seven of school age are not attending at all now. The other extreme is in a family where they do not keep their children out even when the cotton is being ruined from lack of pickers, or in another where they have always considered that school comes before anything else. A family who have recently changed from cotton to tobacco gave as one reason for changing that tobacco can be "housed" before school begins and the stripping can be done without rushing or having to have the help of the children, while cotton required keeping them out a month or so to get it picked. And yet on one visit to this family, two of the children were being kept out from school to "take off" tobacco, "for just a day or two." Another family kept all their children out for two weeks until they finished picking cotton; the older children picked and the younger took care of the baby. A mother who has no girls keeps her boys out once a week to help with the washing. Another mother says they try not to keep their boys out more than three days a month—the maximum allowed if credit for school work is given—but they have been so busy this fall they have had to exceed this limit.

Attitudes toward education come out in connection with the description of practices. The farm-centered mother thinks the only solution would be a six-months' school for country children. As it is they *have* to stay out when they are needed and this practice makes them get behind their town schoolmates (her children go to a consolidated high school in town). Her boys do not like to stay out on account of getting behind and this makes keeping up with the farm work very hard on the aging parents. A tenant who lives in the county where the welfare officer is active does not keep his children out, "because I sure don't want to get put on the road and have a gun pointed at me." He laughed as he gave this reason and said he thought the law was really a good thing because some people would not give their children an opportunity to go to school if they were not made to do so. Just a few miles away another father roundly condemned this law and does not believe it will hold—"The govern*ment* can't tell a man what to do with his children unless it's going to take over the feeding and clothing of them." He believes a nearby Negro who was fined for keeping his children out could have kept from paying the fine if he had held out for his rights.

Another mother in this county keeps hers out only a day or two at the time so that the law cannot get her. She and her husband are tying tobacco at night now, but if they make the children help even at night, they get behind in their school work. And if they get bad marks and do not pass, then it's just eight months wasted and the children do not want to go to school the next year. Whenever the parents want them to do anything the children say, " 'I've got to study for two "testies" tomorrow'—that's all you hear. So I and this here husband of mine work till midnight to get through so they can keep up in school." In some cases it is the child who wants to stay out. An illiterate mother wishes hers would go, "for a person without education nowadays ain't looked on no better'n a dawg—I know because I ain't never had a day's schooling in my life." A boy found staying out to help measure up corn shucked the day before had played sick until too late to go to school that morning, although ordinarily he goes without any trouble. A mother whipped one of her daughters every morning for a month to make her go to school the year she started, and finally had to give it up for that year.

Interesting attitudes were revealed on school matters other than attendance. There is quite general approval of the courses in agriculture and home economics. In one county the three mothers of boys who go to high school said their sons were more interested in and enthusiastic about the agriculture course than they ever had been about anything else in school. One of them will not study or talk about anything else; another has become so interested in it that his mother hopes he is going to change his mind about wanting to leave the farm. A number of garments were proudly displayed by the mothers of girls who had made them in home economics class, and one mother now permits her daughter to use her sewing machine since they have had practice at school.

An attitude not modal, but fairly widespread, is resentment against consolidation and having to send children into town to school. This is based on the unsatisfactoriness of bus service and on the dislike of having children in contact with town children. The first objection is more operative where schedules are cumbersomely arranged; one family of small children have to ride twelve miles to school and are away from home from seven in the morning until five in the afternoon. The mothers claim that their own children learn more "badness" than "goodness" both on the bus and from the town children. One is bitter over her children's hearing the town children talk disrespectfully to their teachers, because they pick up the habit and behave that way at home. Another resents the way country children are snubbed by town children. Among the more isolated rural families there seems to be a reaction against the infiltration of urban patterns from "town" schools similar to that of the first generation immigrants against the Americanization of the second generation. Rural children see town children who do not have to work, who have fine clothes, go to movies, do not mind their parents, and these liberties make them want to behave similarly.

Generally there is interest in the child's achievement in school and pride in good records. Report cards were offered for inspection and one mother glowed as she told of her son's winning a medal for the best all-round student in high school. Another boasted that her daughter had made all 90's after staying out nearly a month in the fall on account of her health. When ages and grades of children are being listed, there is usually an explanation supplied if the retardation is noticeable. The most common reason given for children's having fallen behind is that they have had to stay out because of work, sickness, or because they had no clothes to wear to school. Several blame the placement policy, which puts children back one year if they change schools during the year. This affects many tenants, who, if they move, do so around Christmas time. A few complained of trouble with teachers and explained failing to pass because "you can't learn from anybody you don't like." Some admitted frankly that their retarded children are simply slow in school or "no good at books."

There are not many specific and definite plans for vocations or for formal training after high school. One farmer brags that his son "don't want to have to look at a mule all his life," and a mother, that her son says, "I ain't going to stay on a farm and have it kill me the way it has you all," but there is much vagueness in the parents' plans and even in their hopes for their children. Nearly a third of them want their children to continue farming, while more than half want them to go into something else, because even though some of these think country life is the best, they know how hard it is now to make a living by farming. The others are willing for their children to do whatever they choose or to take whatever jobs they can get. Vocations other than farming and homemaking named as possibilities by parents or children were, for girls, beauty parlor operator, nurse, salesgirl, mill worker, stenographer, and teacher; and, for the boys, truck and bus driver, filling station operator, "business," and preacher.

In only three families was any formal training beyond high school going on: one girl was taking a business course by correspondence, another was at a state college for women, and a boy was at a junior college. A girl who had graduated three years before with the highest record ever made at the village high school had wanted to go to the same junior college, which costs only $200 a session. The preacher tried to persuade her father to send her and pointed out that the $600 he paid that year for a truck would have kept her in school for three years, but the father said there was no use in it—as sure as they spent money on her education she would go get married and then what use would it be? In only one other family was a college education mentioned as being an aim. This young couple with only one child, now five, are planning to limit their family so that they will be able to send him to college, because, they believe, "you have to have education to get anywhere." In speaking of vocations the mothers often said they felt sorry for teachers and were certainly glad they themselves did not have to teach school.

The church, the other institution for training outside of the home, seems to be of diminishing importance. About half of the children go to Sunday School, "but not always regular." The children of one family go in summer but cannot in winter because the four under school age do not have the necessary wraps. One mother would like to have hers go but there is not a church near and they do not have a car. Beyond the fact of attendance at Sunday School, very little information about religious training was obtainable from either the parents or the children. Whatever effect organized religion has upon them is not easily expressed or observed. Instead, Sunday School appears rather to be a routine, to which interest attaches chiefly because it means visiting afterwards. Church services in the neighborhoods visited are rarely more frequent than once a month.

The results of the "raising" can not easily be typified. Of the many children encountered, the most common characteristics observed were an active interest in a stranger and a desire to share the visit. They questioned the visitor about everything from whether she was paid to visit to what she had seen at the State Fair and what books her daughter read. Their manners varied from the conventional courteous forms to a sullen, half-grown boy's coming in without saying a word and lying on a bed in the room in which the visit was taking place. The most striking difference noted between these children and urban ones was their ability to do more sorts of household and farm tasks than urban children, and their apparent willingness to do them.

As has been often observed of rural people, the lives of the tenant group are quite family centered. In tenant families the family pattern has to be based more upon personal relations than in owner families, where there are also ties to land, home, and various acquisitions. In no particular do the portrayals of certain fiction writers seem more unrepresentative than in their belittling of family ties. Many a mother cried over a temporary or permanent loss of a member of her family, but only one over feeling sorry for herself in having such a hard lot. Occasions which made for tears were sons' leaving for CCC camps, another son's moving a mile away now that he is married, another's not having written for a year except for a Mothers' Day card. Bereavement of her children by death seems to be the hardest burden of all that the mother has to bear. Grief over the death of a favorite child, or of the baby who fell in the fire, or of an only little girl, or of a mother's twelfth baby is not in the least diminished because there are many other children left. It seems that more value attaches to children when they represent about all a man and his wife can call their very own. This has a basis beyond their economic value as is demonstrated by the excess of affection showered upon afflicted children; a father spoke for a long time of how he loves his little dumb daughter too much to let her go to an institution; a whole family pets a badly ruptured baby; a stepmother pays especial attention to a child who has fits; various members of one family stop working to roll cigarettes from newspaper and tobacco for a low-grade, feeble-minded child; and an adoring father twice commented on the beautiful eyelashes of his feeble-minded son.

Mothers enjoy telling about raising children and most of them seem well satisfied with the results. "There's one thing I *have* done, I *have* raised my children," was a typical comment with the implication that the job had been well done. Adjudged by some mothers to be the hardest of all their labors, the task of raising is taken by some with unbelievable calm and unconcern. As the two little boys rattled stovewood and frying pans over the floor noisily, a mother nursed her baby while talking with the visitor. Then without stopping either activity, she reached down, grasped the knee-baby by the back part of her clothing, and literally tossed her into a nearby cradle, where she immediately fell asleep. Most of the women recognize child raising as a mother's most serious responsibility and yet they can still treat it humorously, as did a mother who said, "How do I raise my children? I pulls them right up by the hair of their head!"

Chapter 11

Of Wifehood

SOME OF THE husbands were seen and others were described by their wives. Always in overalls, rarely freshly shaved, and reddened from exposure to the weather, they appeared on superficial observation to be more uniform than their wives. They also seemed to be surer of themselves in meeting and conversing with a stranger, although one who drove up in a car was embarrassed to get out because he was barefooted. Without exception, all the husbands met were friendly, somewhat interested and curious, hospitable, and courteous. While the conversation with them was intended to be restricted to farming or related matters, they often broke into that going on with their wives to add information or express opinions. There was no probing or exhaustive exploration into their interests and attitudes, but certain common features appeared in the more or less incidental conversations.

Even though the conversations were intentionally directed towards farming, it was evident that the topic of first importance in tenant farmers' minds is the current crop—how their own is coming along, the effects of the season or pests, and the price it is bringing. Along with their reports were queries about conditions in other counties or farming areas, as from a farmer in a strictly tobacco area, "What are the cotton farmers saying this year?" When the visit was in the striphouse and conversation lulled, the husband, father-in-law, or brother-in-law often assumed a host's responsibility and for entertainment related accounts of previous farming years—the bad year of 1932, the year of the drought, the year when they "shucked out" one hundred and fifty barrels of corn. Sitting in the kitchen on a rainy day, one man was reminded of the year it rained so much that the cotton seed sprouted right in the bolls and ruined all their cotton. It was true of the husbands as of the wives that the unusual and atypical events were the ones remembered and told about rather than everyday routine ones.

There was not a rigid circumscribing of subject matter to agriculture; one man told of his taking the part of Rip Van Winkle in a recent P-T-A play, for which he was qualified because he was such a good sleeper. A number of others talked of their children and their views on education. Another who has a radio installed in his striphouse wanted to talk football although he has never seen a game in his life. Another wanted to discuss the book he was reading, *Daniel Boone, the Pioneer Scout*. The direction of another's interest was inclined to be more personal and flattering; his daughter said he always liked to have women agents visit. "That's a pretty set of teeth *you* have," he commented, while his wife was telling of her dental troubles. After this couple had given the requested information about age and age at marriage, they reciprocated by returning the questions. To a frank reply the man gallantly declared, "You don't look much more than eighteen now—you must of took awful good care of yourself." This may be contrasted with a remark of a mother of six on discovering the visitor was exactly the same age as herself, "I think if you'd dye your hair, you wouldn't look so much older than you are."

The division of labor between the farmer and his wife has already been described from the point of view of what the wife does. The modal pattern is for the woman to do everything inside the house, for the man to occupy himself on the farm, and for both to share the intermediate duties centering around the back yard and relating chiefly to the care of livestock. So far this sounds fairly evenly balanced, but the wife does field work also for about half the year in addition to her traditionally allocated sphere of labors. The return of services she gets from her husband for her farm work is never equal to it in amount. In fact, the modal pattern is no work at all on the part of the husband inside the house, but some consideration for his wife's field labor in the matter of assigning children for household tasks.

Variations from this pattern are common, however. When one woman's asthma forces her to go to bed, her husband cooks for the family and is as handy as can be about doing everything around the house except washing—he says he "can't go that." He is even good about staying with the children on Sundays occasionally, so that his wife can go visit, since she never gets to leave the house during the week. One Sunday when she left, he bathed all the seven children, dressed them, and took them to Sunday School, "and folks said there wasn't another man in the community who would have done it." Another father is more careful than his wife about seeing that their children have on coats and caps when they go out in the cold—"he fusses over them like a setting hen." He never lifts his hand to do housework, however, and his wife never keeps a child to help her at home if he is needed in the field. One man is as interested as his wife in her flowers and was the one who thought to run and move to safety the row of flower pots (lard cans) from the rickety bench in front of their porchless house when a windstorm came up one afternoon. A certain grandfather likes to sit in the kitchen and hold the baby, but he's not good for any help except bringing in wood and water. What relief from housekeeping chores the mother gets is seldom from her husband or any other adult man who may be living with them.

In division of management, planning, and buying, the modal pattern is for the mother to manage inside the house and the father outside, with the exception that he also selects and buys the food. This division is not rigid and all sorts of modifications and variations are to be found. The only practice which is almost universal is that the wife doesn't "tote the pocketbook" and neither she nor her husband thinks it right for a woman to do so. Questions about "planning" for spending sometimes meet with a lack of comprehension of the matter. During the greater part of the year, there is practically no spending to be planned for and even at the time when the crops are sold, so much of the cash must be paid on debts, fertilizer, and food bills incurred throughout the year, that the surplus does not afford material for extensive planning.

The pattern of the husband's buying the groceries is in strong contrast to its urban counterpart. It seems to rest in part on the traditional rôle of the man as literally the "breadwinner" or "provider," and in part on the fact that the one responsible for producing the basic food materials is logically the one to supplement them. The practice is convenient because it is customary for the man to go to town more often than the woman, it being difficult for her to leave at home or take with her all the young children. Finally, the man's control of all finances issues from the heritage of patriarchal family organization. A woman who is not at all a downtrodden wife says she just wouldn't feel right in a grocery store—it's no place for a woman. Another in discussing the planning and buying of groceries said, "I puts that off on John," as if she were relieved not to be bothered with it. Several almost bragged that their husbands also buy the clothes. A common tribute to the husband's taste and shopping ability is, "He pleases me better than I could please myself." One who doesn't go to town often on account of her health writes lists, but even she leaves the planning of the Sunday meat and dessert up to her husband, who buys groceries every Saturday.

Some families who live a considerable distance from stores and have no cars send lists to town by their landlords.

On the other hand, it is generally conceded that women are better bargainers for clothes. "Sam would buy the first thing they showed him if he liked it, without pricing around in other stores." One wife even decides when her husband needs shirts and purchases them for him. A mother often has a cotton or tobacco "patch" from which she gets the proceeds to buy her own and her children's clothes. In most families this is the nearest she comes to any stage of comparative economic independence or autonomy over any part of the farm income. One woman had had so little experience in buying that when her husband gave her $10 to take to town and spend at the end of a good tobacco year, she returned home that night with $9.50. For many families the buying of clothes has been an unimportant matter in the last few years, especially for those on relief who are given "sewing room" clothes.

There were few exceptions to the wife's "not toting the pocketbook." One wife keeps all the money and gives it out to her husband as he needs it. Another reported that she kept it sometimes and her husband sometimes. And yet even the two of highest economic status subscribed to the custom, although one of them added, "Of course, I get whatever I want from it." Of the various economic practices, this one is perhaps the most indicative of where authority rests. Although an old mother claims that her son and daughter-in-law live with her —and not she with them because she is the oldest and has been farming the longest—still, she not only lets her son make all renting arrangements, all marketing decisions and transactions, and pocket all the proceeds, but she thinks such dealings with money are not "womenfolks' business." Another feels that "if the women start toting the pocketbook and taking over the menfolks' business partly, they'll soon make the women do it all and will have them fighting in the next war."

Voting illustrates the division of affairs along sex lines. Over half of the mothers did not vote for reasons varying all the way from thinking it was wicked to "just not ever getting around to it." There was a rather common explanation or justification of voting offered by those who did vote, or by their husbands, and generally agreed to by both. They had not been for women voting at first, but now that women have the vote and *certain* women do vote, it is the duty of good women (who never would have wanted to vote themselves) to vote in order to offset the effect of the others. This certainly bears the earmarks of having originated with a vote-getting politician. One woman admitted that she did not feel it was a woman's place to vote and really didn't care anything about it, but election day is the only time when people come get her in a car and take her somewhere and pay her some attention, and so she certainly goes with them and votes for whom they say. Another said very tactfully that she believes voting is all right for a woman like the visitor, who reads and keeps up with what is going on and knows what she is voting for, but that she herself doesn't have time to waste on "studying menfolks' business" and she does not feel she knows enough about it to vote. A few political items were interspersed with the explanations of voting policies. A mother said she had voted once, for Hoover, but when she saw what happened with her candidate as President, she decided she had made a mistake and never voted again. Another whose husband has WPA work declares she will always vote for Roosevelt because he "saved" them. A few had voted because schools or liquor were at issue and these could give very good temperance talks, but generally local as well as state or national politics are regarded as "menfolks' " affairs.

A strange contradiction to the ordinary limiting of women's vocations was in the account three families gave of women preachers who had been conducting meetings during the past year. They were given unqualified praise by husbands, wives, and children. In one case they declared that the woman was the best preacher they had ever heard and repeated bits of her life and her sermons. The basis for reconciliation of this attitude with the others regarding woman's sphere seems to be that anyone who does "the Lord's work" is exempt from the ordinary restrictions.

Obviously the generally held ideas about woman's place influence the nature of the wife's rôle and her status within the family. Two generalizations are proposed and then substantiating and exceptional evidence offered. First, there is theoretical acceptance of the rightness of male dominance by both sexes. This has as a corollary belief in innate sexual differences in ability, which prescribe divinely decreed different realms of participation. The proposition and corollary are bolstered by the Bible, the ideological heritage, and custom. Secondly, there may occur an almost complete reversal of the theory in practice, with apparently little awareness of its inconsistency with the accepted beliefs; that is, patriarchy prevails in form, but not always in practice.

In negative substantiation of the first proposition, there were very few complaints on the part of the wives about subjection to their husbands. Grievances against husbands on other scores were fairly frequent: "This here husband of mine stays sick all the time and don't do no work," "John has such a rough way with the chldren," "Joe's too easy going," "Walter hangs around at the filling station all the time," "Jim stays on the path a going." In only the few instances relating to sexual relations described below, however, was there indicated dissatisfaction with the wife's place or evidence that she resented domination. The pattern of male domination seems to be too taken for granted to be remarked upon. Several women wished to move to town and get jobs to make some money, but this seemed to be due to the wish to add to the family income rather than to any dissatisfaction over economic dependence upon husbands. The positive substantiation of male dominance is less direct, since it consists of specific practices rather than abstractions about dominance. The specific points such as management of financial affairs have already been described.

The evidence for the second proposition is largely circumstantial, gathered from observation during visits where both husband and wife were present. In a number of families the situations were quite similar—the wife was undoubtedly the stronger personality and "bossed" her husband to some extent, but always within the forms prescribed by tradition. This was not done by the subtle, indirect, flattering, clinging-vine technique which fragile and beautiful women have often used to control men. On the contrary, the exercise of control was quite open; yet there was apparently no recognition by either that the husband was not the lord and master of his household as they claimed. The paradox seems to indicate that in these cases, at least, dominant or ascendant personality traits are stronger in determining active status relations within a family than is the ideology of the cultural heritage. Especially where the wife participates in common activities with her husband, such as field work and tobacco stripping, is there an opportunity afforded for the stronger personality to gain control. Yet there was in none of these cases the logical extension to recognition of equality or to the awarding to the woman any of those privileges traditionally assigned to the favored male.

The attitudes of husband and wife toward each other could be observed only incidentally. The rôles taken by individuals were quite varied. One husband was a fat, jolly man who likes to laugh; therefore, his wife made humorous exaggerations for his entertainment whenever possible and smiled with success when she drew forth peals of laughter from him. He appreciated his wife and swelled with pride as she listed all the sorts of work she does. After telling of a neighboring owner's wife who was sick and had to have so many thousands of dollars spent on her, she said it was a good thing it was not she, for she would have had to die. Her husband contradicted her with, "No, you wouldn't—you wouldn't have took no such enfeebling disease," and laughed heartily with complete trust in her vigor. Another couple, whose relations came nearest to being equalitarian, frequently contradicted each other, but did it gayly and jokingly. To his accusation that she had cooked so much apple pie lately they were sick of it, she countered, "Well, it's your own fault; you won't allow us to have cake when there's fruit on hand to make pies from," and both laughed over it. A humble, flattering, little man is proud of his wife who is twice his size, because she can make the children "step lively" and can work like a man. On the other hand, the contradictions that took place between another couple were tinged with a sharpness and irritability. A woman who has a grievance against the world at large and Mr. Roosevelt in particular for cutting off her husband's veterans' pension and giving it to old people, seems to extend this feeling to her husband also, to whom she always refers with a suggestion of contempt as, "this here husband of mine."

Description of the more intimate relations between husband and wife must be illustrated by the extreme rather than by the ordinary or modal cases. If a woman has a fairly satisfactory sex adjustment with her husband, the chances are slight that she will feel the need to talk about it. In common with many other inquiries, this study suffers from the weakness of having full information on only the pathological sexual situations and scant data on the normal.

An account of extreme cruelty was told by a woman whose husband had been a heavy drinker. One night a few months before the visit he beat her until she was unconscious and then killed himself. The most pathological situation is one where the father has sexual relations with his daughters, especially when his wife is indisposed because of childbirth or illness. His older daughter married and left home about two years ago and since that time he has been having relations with a younger one. She is just ten years old now and when she came home from school, she displayed her crayon drawings and geography workbook as any young child would. Her brother of twelve, however, called attention to the fact that she had on new shoes and that their father bought her twice as many things as any of the rest of them. This mother is very bitter in her resentment against sex and male dominance. She hates her husband most of all for not caring how many babies he makes her have; she knows men can prevent it by stopping, but he will not—"He treats me just like I was a beast."

Two wives complained of their husbands going with other women and one of these described her husband as "the devil incarnate" when he is drunk. Neighbors reported that two other husbands stay in town at night after they sell tobacco and spend their money on liquor and women. Such ventures, however, are quite limited in frequency by economic reasons even for those tenant husbands who wish them. Two more wives showed typically Victorian reactions in describing their feelings toward sex. One has always hated it but has never let her husband get the upper hand of her. She "began right" when she was first married by saying, "Take your hand off me," if her husband bothered her too often. Now since she has arthritis, which makes intercourse painful, he tries to be as considerate as possible and holds off as long as he can—usually two or three weeks. The other told her complete sex history. In her life the lack of sex information before marriage and a traumatic nuptial experience had combined to condition her against sex completely. She supposes she is now like other women after the menopause—that is, she knows what is going on, but she feels nothing (a commonly held notion).

Little can be told, unfortunately, about the better adjustments. In expressing evaluations of their husbands there were several instances where the wives showed so much embarrassment and manifestation of emotion that there was no doubt as to the sincerity underlying the somewhat conventionally phrased tributes. One woman in summing up her life routine of work and children concluded, "Well, it's a busy life. It seems like I've always had little 'uns on my hands ever since I married. But I'm lots better off than most—some women's husbands don't care nothing about the children and drink up all the money and leave their wives to rake and scrape the best they can. I guess I've been lucky about that—about my husband, anyway." Another woman again and again gave a flattering portrayal of her husband's disposition and various virtues in contrast to her own. Another timid one, at the end of an account of financial troubles, shyly assured me, "But I wouldn't swap husbands with any of them rich women—not for all their money."

Wifehood begins early with tenants, for they do not have to wait to accumulate capital or dowry. The age of these mothers ranged from thirteen to twenty-eight with eighteen as the mean age. The most common reason given for the very early marriages was the death of one or both parents. One was afraid she would be an old maid and another just "took the first chance she got," at thirteen—she didn't know why. This last one lived with her husband's parents a few months, as is quite common, but while still thirteen, set up housekeeping alone with her husband of nineteen. A stove, bedstead, table, and a few chairs are the minimum furnishings required. These and other pieces are sometimes donated by parents and sometimes bought by the new husband from the proceeds of a "patch" allowed him by his father. In addition to beginning early, marriages are not often broken by divorce; only one of the tenant mothers was divorced, although two others were separated from their husbands and considering divorces.

The widows and ex-widows always stressed the economic value of a husband. The one left a widow at twenty-four with four children farmed and managed to keep them alive for eight years, but she doesn't see how the children lived through it with the little they had to eat. Small wonder that at thirty-two she married a boy of nineteen who has "sure made things easier for me." Another widow was able to go back to her parents to live with her children until she found another husband. A woman who was widowed this year laments her lot loudly. Her older children are married and gone and she has left only one son and one daughter who are "fitten" to work. Her son of nineteen is permanently crippled with "bones just like old rotten wood," her father-in-law is too old and feeble to work, and she herself weighs over two hundred and can't get around any more. She thinks the Lord chastises a woman when he takes her husband. Three other widows have received Aid to Dependent Children grants, but they still always mention the loss of a supporter as a cause for grief.

The two mothers who have never had husbands are living at home with slight chances of getting married. Incest was suspected by welfare officials in both cases although the girls claimed differently. Their children seem to be fully accepted into the family and are objects of the devotion and petting usually accorded to the "baby" of the family by all its members.

In summary we may comment upon the apparent lack of friction and irritability between most of the couples, both as observed and as reported by the wife. There was the impression that the sharing of field and barn work and of farming interests made for a spirit of cooperation and an absence of sexual antagonism. Furthermore, in lives where work takes most of one's time, there is little opportunity to contemplate or argue over rights and privileges. None of the wives appeared to be neurotic; none claimed to be misunderstood.

Chapter 12

Of Community Participation

The terms "this neighborhood" and "this community" are used interchangeably by the tenant women to refer to the area within two or three miles of their homes and to the people living in it. Since this study is concerned chiefly with individuals and families, no effort has been made to delimit neighborhoods or communities or to make intensive investigations of their functioning. Our interest in them is from the point of view of their influence on tenant families and especially of the mothers' participation in their activities. We are adopting the tenant farm usage of the words to mean a locality of two or three miles radius, within which most of the people know one another's names, at least, and are not prevented by geographical distance from visiting and having primary associations with one another.

The general policy was not to visit mothers who lived close together, because it was felt that they would give more confidential information if they knew there was no danger of its being repeated to some near neighbor. Therefore, in about half of the neighborhoods only one mother was seen. In the others, two to six mothers were visited because some suggested or even insisted that visits be made to a nearby relative or friend who liked company, and because referrals were often concentrated in certain localities.

These neighborhoods represent all degrees of isolation and availability. One is eighteen miles from "town," another less than two miles, while the mean distance of all houses from town is nine miles. However, few are more than three miles from a store, with a mean distance of about a mile and a half. Over a sixth of the houses are on paved highways, nearly a half on improved dirt roads, usually gravel, and nearly a third on unimproved. Some of these last are plantation or wagon roads which are impassable for automobiles and others are passable only in dry weather. Almost the only locational aspect common to all the families is that they all live in the open country, rural-farm area; referrals to tenants living in villages were discarded.

Mobility makes neighborhood ties and control less operative upon tenants than upon owners. The mean number of years lived in the house now occupied by the tenant family is four, but this is weighted greatly by a few who have lived all their lives in one place. The median time is shorter. The mean number of years the mothers have lived in the community is fourteen and in the county, twenty-four. Almost two-thirds of the women preferred the community in which they are now living to any other. As might be expected, those who have remained in one place a long time are the ones who are best satisfied. Several of these quoted, "There's no place like home." The order of frequency of reasons given for community preference were home (or "We're used to it," or "We was brought up here"), people, convenience, rurality (as contrasted with a town or mill village), and land. The movers have more basis for comparative evaluations and they often contrast "this community" with another differing in time or space, or both. "They just don't visit here," or "Folks don't visit the way they used to," was the most common sizing up of the difference. One woman is very glad to be back in her home community after eight years in several other localities where "folks didn't know what it meant to be neighbors." Some followed up the general criticism, "This just ain't like the community we used to live in," with specific accounts of cooperation, friendliness, and local customs. Others, when pressed for details, showed by their vagueness that the "Golden Age" or "back in the old days" aura was responsible for some of the discontent. This sensing that change in neighborhood life is occurring and that it is to be deplored is a modal attitude.

The church is still the chief organization in which rural people participate. And yet about three-fourths of these tenant mothers do not attend regularly and only three go every Sunday, although almost all go occasionally and to revival meetings in the summer. Only two are engaged in church activities other than mere attendance. Many remarks indicate a consciousness of change here, too. One contrasted her father's reading the Bible and having prayers daily with her own lack of going to church. It seems that she is always pregnant or has a child too young to take. A half dozen women alluded to the former practice of taking a quilt and making a pallet in the aisle for the baby to sit or sleep on, but no one of them does this now. A mother who deplores the fact that there is no church in her community thinks all the children nearby are growing up just like heathen with no Sunday School to go to.

There seems to be little violent denominational loyalty although denominations still have some importance even to those who do not go to church. A Presbyterian who lives in a Baptist and Methodist community has evidently suffered from discrimination, for she said apologetically that she thought Presbyterians were as good as anybody even if there were not so many of them. A woman and her children go to the Baptist church while her husband goes to the Methodist since he was turned out of the Baptist church for not paying his part of the pastor's salary—or so the treasurer alleged, although the husband claims he did pay it. This same husband asked his wife to join the Methodist church with him, but she wants to stay in the Baptist where she was brought up and feels more at home, although she does not think the difference in beliefs among denominations amounts to anything. There was only one woman who wanted to engage in a theological discussion. A Missionary Baptist, when she "got to studying about" close communion, was worried because she feels that "all God's children should partake together." Later her pastor came and talked with her about it so that she feels much better over the matter now, although she couldn't tell exactly how he explained away her difficulties.

The preacher is still regarded as a specially privileged dignitary; this was indicated by references to the sort of food he must have, by the importance attached to his saying contraception was not a sin, and by the fact that the children in one family reproached their mother for mentioning whipping them in his presence. However, only one mother cherishes the hope that her son will become a minister. Her little boy of ten wants to be one but he is afraid he "hasn't lived right"; he fights at school sometimes and once told his teacher a lie when, to get permission to go to the basement, he said he had taken medicine. Into such personal, anecdotal avenues discussion of church or religion generally leads. The evidences of orthodox ideology appear more frequently in an indirect way in the form of moralizations to "round off" any account of behavior or even any opinions that need to be bolstered.

The two other organizations to which some of these mothers belong are the Parent-Teacher Association and the local home demonstration clubs. Membership is not the modal pattern, however, as only about ten percent belong to either. Usually it is the "upper crust" of the tenant group who participate in these; the three most prosperous women are quite active in money-raising projects of the P-T-A and are grade mothers. Since consolidation, distance from school limits participation for many. One tries to go occasionally by catching a ride in and coming back on the school bus because she feels the teachers will take more interest in her children if she shows that much interest in them.

Some of the home demonstration agents in these counties say that usually only the "highest class" tenant women belong to their clubs although the agents make every effort to keep the club work on a democratic basis. One mother who has lived in a community a long time told proudly of the club house her group had built and added that all the rest of the members were owners' wives. Several tenant women, however, go regularly and one has had the meeting at her own house. She also was one of those who went to the county seat to petition the commissioner to get a full-time agent. In her club the division is on a political rather than social class basis. Only Democrats come to their meetings although they have invited the Republicans, and politics is never discussed. The ex-school teacher is chairman of the garden committee of her club. Another used to go to a home demonstration club but it died out because people did not have time for it. This was the most common excuse for nonattendance in the localities where there were clubs, with care of children, field work, or "not having anybody to leave to take care of the house," as specific reasons. Only one woman whose husband is treasurer of a Masonic lodge goes into a village chapter of the Eastern Star.

"Just visiting" continues to be the chief extra-home social activity in spite of its constantly attested decline. Only twelve women reported that they did no visiting although nearly three times this many said they visited very little. One woman said no neighbor had entered her home for a year. Another, living in a very inaccessible location, had had no company during the five months she had lived there and said her baby had never seen a stranger before. Mothers who live near their own families generally report the most visiting, and interview visits were often shared with relatives. Sunday is the chief day for visiting—especially family visiting—and some member of a family who has a car often comes for those who haven't or brings others to see them. An interesting aspect of country social life is the cutting across conventional age limits for association. Many young girls who can leave home more easily than their mothers frequently visit mature women neighbors. Sometimes they help with household tasks, and sometimes they just talk, often telling news which the more mobile can collect and share with the ones tied down. The same excuses are given for not visiting more as for not attending church and clubs: "too busy," pregnancy, children, and no means of transportation.

Only one mother goes to dances and they are the square ones her husband plays his guitar for every now and then. She was brought up not to dance and never would go when she was first married. After about six years her husband tricked her one night and got her to dress herself and the three children up to go "visiting" at a neighbors. She had no idea a dance was to be there and was surprised when people started coming in. Since she was already there she let them persuade her to stay and she enjoyed it. Except for this one, no mother told of going to parties or gatherings expressly for social purposes other than family reunions. An occasional church supper, an oyster stew for the benefit of the school, or a cooperative project was the nearest to purely social functions. Very few mentioned going to movies.

The most widespread occasion for gatherings of a semisocial nature is the cornshucking. Cornshuckings were reported in many of the more settled, stable neighborhoods and variations and trends were described. Formerly the women always went to help cook and sometimes to quilt while the men shucked, but this practice is fading. Perhaps one or two close neighbors come in to help but the mother often has to hire a colored woman since usually only men come now. The modal pattern is for the men to come early in the "evening," work until supper time, have served to them chicken or brunswick stew, cabbage, and pie or cake, either outdoors or inside at successive tables, and go back and continue to shuck until bedtime. One family had so much corn this year that they had to give the shuckers dinner and supper. Some people do not give meals but invite only men and supply a keg of whisky. This is passed around before work begins and every hour or two afterward so that the guests will get just enough to make them work without getting drunk. This incentive is often used if Negroes are to be asked in, for it removes the matter of eating, which could not be done together and, "you can get niggers to do *any*thing for a drink or two."

There is an obligation to go to every man's cornshucking who comes to yours. A story was told on one of the women by her brother. Alice was always the best woman in the community about going to help with the cooking whenever anybody had a cornshucking. She was so good about it that when she and her husband had theirs, all the women she had helped came to help her in return. What a cornshucking! There were about twenty-five women to cook and only two or three men to be cooked for, since the others had stayed at home with the children so their wives could come. (Women never help with the actual shucking.) Alice said she would never go to help another woman again if that was the way it turned out. In other families they shuck out the corn themselves, a little at a time; often the children work on it every afternoon when they get home from school. Several who still have shuckings believe this would be more economical because one could shuck his own during the time he spends going to other people's shuckings and he saves the expense of feeding fifteen to twenty-five men. But since "it seems easier when you're working together," quite a few continue along the traditional lines.

The cornshucking is the form of cooperative endeavor most commonly reported, but other phases of farm work are sometimes done similarly. In one neighborhood the families grade tobacco separately during the day and at night they go around from one striphouse to another tying together. If a man is sick in this locality, a neighbor goes right out and plows for him or gets his crop in. In another farmers do a number of things together: picking up potatoes and even picking cotton so that they can all be working together in a crowd. Woodchoppings, housepaintings, and "thrashings" were mentioned rarely. Fairly often tenants on the same farm work "through and through," or "backwards and forwards," which means they all work on one man's field and then all on another's. Occasionally this is done throughout the year, but more often for only parts of the season. Several farmers told of communities in which they had lived where several families would "save their crop" together. Where barns are close together, one man can keep going and tend the fires of several people. One farmer has tried this but says he prefers doing his own by himself—if he goes to sleep then, no one's tobacco is ruined but his own and nobody has ruined it for him but himself. "Swapping work" in general is reported to be on the decline.

Direct questions were not employed in getting at race and class attitudes, but references to such matters and expressions indicative of attitudes were carefully noted. It must be remembered that the tenant-landlord class cleavage is not the only dichotomy possible; there are also the rural-urban and the black-white divisions. Furthermore, so far as could be determined, none of the neighborhoods had been visited by farm union organizers or exposed to propaganda directed toward the developing of class consciousness. This very lack of inculcation of ideas upon the tenants by outsiders lends interest to the content of their thinking along these lines.

We consider first the two divisions other than that of owner-tenant. Without exception every reference to Negroes was in keeping with the traditional patterns. Even the one woman born outside of the South had adopted the regional prejudices during her ten years' residence. Twice there was delay in finding houses because in giving directions the woman had ignored the Negro houses as if they did not exist. The "third house on the left" meant the third "white" house. A mother describing the neighborhood where she has lived all her life was puzzled when asked about a schoolhouse a mile and a half down the road. She stated positively that there was no schoolhouse on the road mentioned. When the location was carefully specified, she laughed and said, "Oh, that's a nigger school—I knew there wasn't any school on that road." Another mother confided what she considered the worst thing she had ever heard about anybody—that a family she knows let a Negro hand eat right at the table with them.

Another detail of the traditional pattern is the white woman's fear of the Negro man. In the three or four cases where the woman claimed fear on account of isolation, she said it was because of the danger of Negro men. Two of them told of cases they had heard of where Negro men had killed white women. The one who never lets her family leave her alone either day or night because of this fear is the one who controls her granddaughter with threats to let the Big Black Nig get her. She says the threat does not work so well on this child as it used to on herself when she was a little girl. Several stated they did not approve of leaving one's children with "niggers" to be taken care of. Of course, none of the mothers had regular house servants. There were a number of mothers who expressed commendation or regard for individual colored women, usually "grannies," but there was no mistaking the "in their places" qualification to any regard for them. A mother is moving into a house where colored people have been living this year, but as it is much better than her present one she did not indicate any resentment over its former occupancy. At a filling station a tenant man loudly condemned the practice of permitting Negroes to attend the State Fair (on a day set aside for them) and wanted to get rid of them all. From the mothers, however, there were no such violent expressions of race prejudice.

Second only to this recognition of separation from Negroes is the awareness of differences from "town people," which is extended to include all people from any place other than a Southern farm. In many cases there was a noticeable increase of confidence after the visitor explained she was "brought up" in the country and often there were remarks such as, "Well, you know how it is, then," or "I didn't think you seemed like a town person, even if you have got nice clothes," or "I told John I felt at home with you the very first time you came." One aspect of this feeling has been illustrated in connection with sending children to consolidated schools in town. One mother thinks the old-fashioned country schools are better and that country children "don't need no fanciness in their schooling." The belief is prevalent that "town" women make poor wives for farmers because, as one mother said of her daughter-in-law, "she don't know *nothing*." Most emphasized of all is the attitude that the country is the only place "to bring up children right," that children in town are not brought up right and are bad influences. One mother deplores the fact that her grown daughters want to go into town whenever they can "catch a ride" whether they have any money to spend or not. Another is bitter against "town creeping out on the country," a condition she thinks the filling stations are largely responsible for. With very few exceptions the mothers preferred living in the country and usually stated such a preference with some derogatory comment about towns such as "People are so jammed up in mill towns."

References to people more foreign than the inhabitants of nearby towns were rare, for they are simply not within the experience content of these tenants. The diet of Canadians was severely criticized by a mother whose son had gone to Canada to cure tobacco this summer. A woman who once spent six months in "the North" while her husband had a job in West Virginia disliked the people heartily because, "I couldn't understand them and they couldn't understand me." The only reference to those of other than the Protestant faith was made by the religious mother when she qualified her assertion that "All God's children should partake together," with a hasty, "of course, I've never known any Jews or Catholics." One farmer criticized academicians when he complained about Roosevelt's putting them in positions of importance. He thinks it will ruin the country because "them college professors don't know nothing but books."

In expressions of social class or landlord-tenant attitudes, both content and degree of explicitness varied considerably by neighborhoods. There is everywhere an awareness of separation from the owning class. With any remark about a neighbor, there was generally an identifying of status if he were an owner: "Mrs. S.—her husband owns the next place—" or "The B. family, they own their own place." The next step in the development of class consciousness—the identification of one's self with others of similar economic status leading to a "we" feeling and finally to a unity of purpose culminating in collective endeavor toward the betterment of the class—is not nearly so prevalent. Its beginnings are present in certain individuals, however, and may be illustrated by grievances against landlords reported by either husband or wife. These include accusations of crookedness, of cheating, of holding out AAA and Soil Conservation checks, of raising rent when the tenant improves the land, and, most common of all, of being "tight," in one case so "tight" he charged $5.00 for the use of his car on a five-mile trip to the graveyard, in another case so "tight" he tried to collect a half of the fish and game a man got on Saturday afternoons and Sundays.

Generalization of instances of social and economic discrimination into a theory or systematic body of principles has not proceeded very far. "Them as owns looks down on them as rents," "Folks around here is too biggity," "They ain't no need for tenants to go to court," and "Things is unbalanced and the poor don't get their share," are about as far as the tenant mothers go in thinking the matter through. One rather common stereotyped complaint about working on halves is that "you work one day for yourself and the next for the landlord and he should at least feed you on the day you work for him."

A number of these tenant families were on very small holdings where the owner lived nearby and operated his own farm. In these situations, status differences are minimized and there are more often than not reports of neighborly practices and friendliness. On larger plantations the tenant may assume some standing because of the prestige of the owner. One mother is very proud that they are on the place of a man who is the "stoutest" man in the county. She sang his virtues and gave concrete examples of his goodness in inviting all his tenants to his birthday party last year and of his wife's in bringing them medicine. Such paternalistic practices seem still to be effective in keeping the tenant in a "landlord's tenant" rôle analogous to that of a "white man's nigger." On another large plantation there were expressions of loyalty to the absentee owner, even though the manager was so detested that twelve of the families were moving at the end of the year. In incidental contacts with landlord's wives, there were more explicit statements of class feeling, accompanied by characterizations of tenants as shiftless and ignorant and the most common charge, that they spend their money foolishly.

From the tenant mothers there were many tales of hardship, of the hopelessness of getting ahead, of "what a farmer has to expect," and references to themselves as poor people. The projection of blame for their economic plight, however, is not usually focused upon the owner. It is rather on the general system which does not allot to the agricultural division of production its fair share. One mother blames it on prices—"There's no jest (justice) in prices anyway—fat meat twenty-two cents a pound in the store and cotton bringing only nine!" They offer no thought-out solution for the situation and some ventured the opinion that nobody knew what to do about it, not even the government. Some few tie it up with the traditional individualism of the farmer so often manifested in statements like, "I don't love to have nobody tell me what to plant or how to run my place." A seventy-five-year-old ex-tenant farmer who had worked a few years in a factory best put the idea of unionization into words. He was summarizing his life's work and the prospects for farming: "Farming is the sweetest work man ever done. It's the most important thing of all. It's like the main wheel going around, and I say if it was to stop, everything would be stopped. But the farmers don't get their share—here's cotton only nine cents a pound now. They never will get their share because they won't organize like manufacturing workers—you couldn't *get* 'em to organize, even if they knew they'd get more, because each one wants to do his own way and won't have nobody telling him how to manage his business."

Chapter 13

Of the Tenant Child as Mother to the Woman

So FAR WE HAVE presented pictures of the tenant farms on which the mothers live and work, and then topical descriptions of their various activities. In a later chapter we shall give a summary of quantitative data to orient this group in the larger one of Southern tenant farm mothers. And yet something more is needed if we are to understand the realism of all that this means to the mothers themselves and to the Region. This something else must be found somehow in a richer portrayal of how these mothers live, move, and have their being.

It is possible to do this through a sort of magnified case portraiture which offers still another way of looking into the mothers' lives. This affords opportunity to observe the continuity of change and development wrought in an individual by long time exposure to the environmental factors subsumed under "Southern farm tenancy." For instance, the annals of the life of Mollie Goodwin unfold to reveal much that goes into the making of the tenant farm mother's world.

The story of the tenant child begins more than a quarter of a century ago. On Monday ten-year-old Mollie woke up when her mother lifted the stove lid and began making the fire. She slipped from underneath the cover easily, so as not to disturb her little brother, and took down her last year's red dress, which had been fleecy and warm, but now was slick and thin. Their bed was in the log kitchen of the Goodwin's two-room cabin, which would be warm enough in a half hour for the sickly knee-baby, who slept with Mollie, to face the December morning.

Mollie's father came from the main room of the cabin to lace up his shoes in front of the kitchen stove. He never made the fire unless his wife was sick in bed, but he got up at the same time she did to go out to the smokehouse and measure out the day's allowance of meat. Ben Goodwin was a saving man who could not abide waste. He made his share of the proceeds from the small, cotton tenant farm buy the annual fall clothing supply for his family of seven and run them through the winter and spring until midsummer or later. Even then, he kept his account at the country store the lowest of any family's in the neighborhood, doing all the buying himself and measuring out the rations every morning.

Mollie's plump arms stretched tight the seams of her outgrown dress, and as she leaned over to pick up fresh wood for the fire, she felt her dress split at the shoulder. She wondered what she would do the washing in if she couldn't get into the old dress next Monday or the one after that. Her father's rule was that her two new dresses of the same cotton fleece lined material, one red and one blue, must never be worn except for school or Sunday School. She had no sisters to hand down clothes to her, for the other four children were boys. Some girls she knew wore overalls for working, but her father would not allow that either. A wicked thought came to her mind—maybe if she had nothing to wear to wash in next Monday, she wouldn't have to wash and instead could go to school with her brothers. She could iron on Tuesday inside the house in her underwear—then a vision of her mother bending over the wash tubs, moaning with the pain in her back, made her put aside the daydream of a washless Monday.

After breakfast Mollie's older brother cut wood and started a fire under the wash pot while she and the brother next younger drew and carried water from the well. Then the boys left for the mile walk to the one-teacher school and Mollie started back for the house to get up the clothes. She lingered on the way, debating whether her father's overalls, stiff with a week's accumulation of winter mud and stable stains, were harder to wash than the baby's soiled diapers. They *were* harder, but the odor from the diapers made you feel you couldn't go on. It was a sensory symbol of babies, of her sick mother, of crying, little brothers, and now was vaguely mixed with her distaste for what two girl friends had told her at recess last week about how babies come. Mollie tried not to think about this and hoped she never had any babies.

The school bell's ringing interrupted her musing and reminded Mollie of how much she wanted to be there. Her dress was as new as any in school and its color still bright. The teacher had smiled approvingly at Mollie last week when the visiting preacher pinched her dimpled cheek and said, "Miss Grace, you have a fine looking bunch of little girls." Mollie thought now of having, when she was grown, a dress like Miss Grace's Sunday one. The bell stopped ringing and Mollie resolved to stop thinking and to work very hard and fast. Once before she had finished all the washing in time to go back with the boys after dinner. And so she scrubbed with all her force against the washboard and paid no attention to the pain from her knuckles scraped raw.

By dinner time all the clothes were on the line and the first ones out already frozen stiff. Mollie, numbed by cold and fatigue, ate peas, fat pork, and cornbread without joining in the family talk. When she got up from the table, her back ached—she wondered how many years of washing it would take to make it as bent over as her mother's. She changed to her new dress in time to set off for the afternoon session of school. She pulled herself together to respond to the teacher's beaming look of approval for having come to school that afternoon, and then relaxed into a lethargy from weariness and missed words she knew in the Third Reader and was spelled down quickly.

Back at home after school, the older boys went out to shuck corn. The Goodwins had decided not to have a cornshucking this year since the boys were getting big enough to be able to get it done after school hours. Then, too, the mother was unable to cook for a crowd and there were no pigs or chickens to spare to feed a hungry bunch of working men. Mollie worked in the house sweeping and straightening while her mother lay on the bed and told her what to do.

Mollie's play had to be largely with her brothers because the only close neighbor had no daughters. In summer she would go to the creek with them and, if no other boys were along, go in swimming with them, too. The boys wore nothing but she wore her oldest dress. They were good to her and often let her play ball with them. Once in the spring the three children stayed after school to watch a baseball game and when they got home at dark, Ben Goodwin was beside himself with anger. They had neglected work and had watched a baseball game, which was against his religious principles. He whipped them all severely, even Mollie. They never went to a baseball game again.

On Sundays Ben walked to Sunday School with his four oldest children and waited outside to go home with them. Sometimes his brother's family joined them for Sunday dinner and Mollie got to play with girls on those afternoons. Their game was "Mama and Papa," "ma' like," or "playhouse." They went out into the pasture and gathered moss for beds and rocks for bureaus. With broken glass and china they completed furnishing the playhouses in which they preacted out their lives. Mollie, always interested in her looks, found curly shavings of wood and stuck them in her hair, pretending she had long ringlets. The older boys sometimes helped collect the accessories for playing house, but they left when the imaginative narration began and the girls were reduced to using their baby brothers for husbands.

Mollie liked summer time best after the cotton had been chopped, hoed, and laid by. Once or twice a week she was allowed to go spend the afternoon with Mrs. Bynum, the nearest neighbor, who had no daughters. They sat on the front porch and rocked and talked. This was a treat for the little girl because her own mother always had to lie down when she could stop working, and pain limited her words to necessary instructions. One summer Mrs. Bynum bought some flowered dimity and made Mollie a visiting dress. They used to hitch up her horse to the buggy and drive four miles to visit a sister who had twelve children, most of them girls. The older girls let Molly try on hats and brooches and Mollie loved these afternoons. On the trip Mrs. Bynum taught Mollie to drive the horse. In her own family's wagon there were always boys who claimed this privilege.

One stormy winter night three months before Mollie was twelve, she was put to bed early. Her father moved the trundle bed from the main room and all the children went to sleep in the kitchen—all but Mollie. She had a terrible feeling of impending disaster to her mother and herself. When she had asked her mother about babies not long before, her mother had told her she was going to have another and that something would happen to Mollie soon, too. From the front room Mollie heard groans and knew her mother was suffering. Her own body began to ache. Her mother's sounds grew louder and each time an anguished scream reached Mollie's ears, a shooting pain went through her. Hardly daring, Mollie reached down under the cover and felt that her legs were wet. All the boys were asleep and so she drew back the cover and in the moonlight saw black stains which had come from her body. Suddenly she thought she was having a baby. She tried to scream like her mother, but the terror of the realization paralyzed her. Fright overwhelmed her until she was no longer conscious of pain. She remained motionless for a long time, knowing and feeling nothing but a horrible fear of disgrace and dread. Then she became aware that the moaning in the next room had stopped and that someone had unlatched the kitchen door. Trembling, she eased out of bed and crept into her mother's room. There was a new baby lying on one side, but she slipped into the other side of the bed and nestled against her mother. The relaxing warmth and comfort of another's body released the inner tensions and Mollie melted into tears and weak, low sobs. Her mother stroked her but said nothing. She lay there for some minutes until the Negro "granny" said she must leave her mother and led her back to bed. Early in the morning she hid the soiled bedclothes in a corner until she could wash them secretly in the creek and found some cloths in her mother's drawer which she asked for without giving any reason. Not for two years, when a girl friend told her, did she have any instruction about how to fix and wear sanitary pads.

The summer Mollie was fourteen her mother persuaded Ben to buy her a silk dress. Mollie had worked so well that year that her father, in an appreciative mood, took her to town and let her select the material, which was a glamorous, changeable, rose and green taffeta. Mrs. Bynum helped her make it, and when her father consented to take the whole family to a Fourth of July celebration ten miles away, Mollie's cup overflowed with joy. She rolled up her hair in rags the night before. She helped bathe and dress the younger children two hours before leaving time so that she might extract the full delight from dressing leisurely in her new clothes for the first time. By eight o'clock in the morning, the family, now nine, piled into the wagon and set off. To keep from going through the county seat, they cut through a shorter, back road, which was rocky and went over steep hills. The boys got out and pushed on the worst places, but Mollie sat on the bench with her mother and father—accorded special privileges because of her new dress. The jolting and hot sun bearing down were unnoticed for the joy anticipated in being the most beautifully dressed girl at the celebration. Mollie was scarcely aware of her family in the wagon as she rode along with her head in the clouds.

They reached the tabernacle, where there were to be political speeches interspersed with hymn singing contests between churches. Mollie hopped down lightly and was about to run over to join a group of girls she knew when her mother, climbing over the edge of the wagon more slowly, called her back and took her a few steps away from the wagon.

"Your dress is ruined behind," she whispered to Mollie, "you'll have to set still over here by this tree all day." Excitement and the jolting had brought on her menstrual period early and the realization of this brought about a flush of hot shame which obliterated the festive scene of picnic tables and merry people. Mollie's heart seemed to close up and with it her capacity to perceive or respond. Passively she allowed herself to be led to a sheltered spot under an oak with protruding roots which afforded a seat. The loss of her life's triumph and the indescribable embarrassment kept her from comprehending meanings. She felt that she was dead and after awhile she leaned against the tree and slept. No one approached, for there seemed to be a tacit understanding of her plight. Late in the afternoon she rode home without speaking to her family. The next day she and her mother were unable to remove the stain from her dress and the beautiful taffeta was never worn. Her father never bought her another silk dress.

Two years later, Mollie finished the seventh grade at sixteen. The other girls were now having boys drop by their houses, but Ben Goodwin was known for his sternness and none came to see Mollie. Johnny Wilson walked home from Sunday School with her, but left her at the turning before the house came into view. Her uncle saw the two together once and quickly carried the report to her father. Ben Goodwin stormed and paced the floor. Finally he said that he would not whip Mollie this time, but that if she ever again spoke to any boy—much less one whose mother was a bastard—he would beat her till he knocked out of her head all those ideas about running around. He never let her have parties or go to those in the neighborhood. Every other girl occasionally invited all the young folks around once each season on Saturday night to play drop the handkerchief and kissing games and to drink lemonade or eat ice cream. Sometimes Mollie's mother helped her to arrange to spend the night with a girl friend on these evenings so she could go to the party from another house. The fear of Ben's finding out about the deception limited these times, and since she had no party dresses, she cared little about going when she could not dress so well as the others.

Only once did a boy ever come to her house. Mollie was sitting on the sills of an unfloored porch which was being added to the house when he rode up one Sunday afternoon on a gray horse. She thought he was looking for her cousin, whose name was beginning to be linked with his, and chatted with him casually. In a few minutes her father appeared at the door and with no preliminary remarks shook his fist at the boy and said,

"Do you see that road? Well, get on your horse and get going on it and don't never come back here again!"

Mollie defended herself, "He's not *my* sport, he's Blanche's," but her father would not discuss it. Word of the event spread around and no other young man ventured to call. Ben Goodwin allowed Mollie to have no more dresses except of the coarsest denim in order to keep highfalutin' ideas from her head.

That summer one of Mrs. Bynum's many nieces went to a town in another county to work in a tobacco factory and her sister reveled in telling Mollie about the money she made and spent. They planned what sort of things Mollie could buy if she were to go to work in town. After weeks of whispered plans, the sister in town arranged for Mollie to have a job weighing and wrapping cigarettes. Without telling even her mother, Mollie bundled up her clothes and left early one morning, just as the cotton picking season was beginning. A neighbor boy drove her to town and she went to a relative of Ben's to board.

For four months Mollie worked in the tobacco factory and exulted in making $20 a week. This was during the post-war boom period and labor was scarce. As fast as the money came in, she spent $15 for a coat, $11 for hightop shoes, $8 for a hat, and smaller amounts for slippers, dresses, beads, and brooches. There were five other women boarding in the same house and Mollie's greatest delight was in the just-before-bedtime lunches they shared. Each one chipped in a nickel every night for cheese, crackers, and fancy canned things. Mollie had never before eaten "store bought" food and had never had even one cent to spend on self-indulgence. After she had bought an entire outfit of new clothes, she went to a county fair with the women. A boy who worked in the cigarette factory asked her to go with him, but she thought she would have a better time with the other women. This boy always hung around Mollie in the factory and said things she thought were fresh, but the landlady wouldn't allow her to go out with him. Once in December he asked Mollie to marry him but she laughed and said, "Why should I marry and keep house and have babies when I've got such a good job and can buy myself such fine clothes?"

Just before Christmas Ben Goodwin got someone to write a letter to Mollie for him. He told her she had to come back home, but that he would make arrangements for her to live during the week with an aunt in the county seat so that she could go to high school in town. Mollie cried and at first said she wouldn't go, but in the end she knew she had to mind her father. She spent her last week's wages buying presents for all the family and went home on Christmas Eve. The next day her mother took flu and one by one the children came down with it. The weakly brother's flu went into pneumonia and finally into tuberculosis, which required so much waiting on that Mollie didn't get to start to school after all.

The following summer Mollie's mother gave birth to her ninth child. It was in the daytime and the baby came in a hurry. No one was in the house except Mollie and the sick brother in the back room. Ben had gone for a doctor but not soon enough and the doctor did not get there in time. The suffering woman begged for help but Mollie did not know what to do. She even pled with Mollie to kill her and put an end to her tortures. Finally the baby was born, but with the covers pulled up so that Mollie could not see. The mother wrapped the baby up and let it lie there until the doctor came and cut the cord.

⁂

With a sick brother, a sickly mother, and a new baby in the house, Mollie had a busy summer. About the only times she had off from household duties were when she spent the night with her cousins or with Mrs. Bynum's nieces. On one such night the young people all went to watch a Negro revival meeting. While they were standing on the outside listening to the shouting through the windows, a man who knew some of the boys came up and joined them. His name was Jim and he was ten years older than Mollie, but he "took a shine" to her from their first meeting. For the rest of the summer he rode his mule for nine miles to come to see her whenever she could spend a night away from home, as Ben was still adamant about no sports coming to his house.

In the fall the brother was better and the original plan for Mollie to go to school in town was feasible. Because Ben had no buggy of his own, and because he wished so much to have his favorite daughter at home on week-ends, he finally consented for Jim to drive her out on Fridays and back to town on Sundays. His mule was the fastest one for miles around, but walked very slowly when Jim was taking Mollie home. This was when they did their courting, for Jim was never permitted to linger after delivering Mollie to her parents. He pressed his suit with urgency, for he was nearly thirty and felt it was time for him to be getting married. Mollie wasn't enjoying going back to school after being out for a year, since she was older than the town girls in her grade and felt awkward with them. She liked Jim although she never felt gay or excited with him the way she did with younger boys. She still did not want to think of marrying and settling down to repeat her mother's life—ruining her health and looks with overwork and childbearing. She made one last appeal to her father to let her go back to work in the cigarette factory, for her one-time job has remained to this day a symbol of money for clothes and luxuries. Ben would not consent, however; he said that factories were no place for his womenfolks and that she could never go back. And so Mollie gave Jim a lukewarm "yes" and they planned to marry on Christmas Day.

Only the day before Christmas Eve did Mollie tell her father she was going to get married. She delayed breaking the news because she expected a violent outburst, although she was eighteen now and "free" and thoroughly determined to marry anyway. Ben surprised her by reacting with more sadness than anger and merely answering, "All right—if you love him more than you do me, go ahead." The next day he went to town and bought her a brown hat for a wedding present, while his wife helped Mollie steam her last year's tricotine dress and put her things in order. On the day of the wedding Ben was up and gone before anyone else awoke and stayed in the woods all day, so as not to be at home when Mollie left. A friend lent Jim a Model T Ford and with two other couples, he and Mollie rode to another town, where he had been hauling during the winter. They had a preacher come to the house of some of Jim's friends to marry them and that night they drove out in the country to Jim's aunt's, where all his people were. They had a big supper with three tables full of people and many kinfolks spending the night. Mollie got more and more embarrassed as the evening wore on, wondering where everybody would sleep. Finally Jim's aunt took her into a room saved just for them and put her to bed and blew out the light.

Jim came in after a few minutes and undressed in the dark and they spent their wedding night very conscious of whisperings and giggles from their relatives in adjoining rooms.

The next night all the young people in the neighborhood had heard of the wedding and came to "shivaree" the newly married couple. They began by making weird noises at the window with tin cans and rosin strings. Jim got up quickly and was nearly dressed by the time they burst the door open. The "shivareers" grabbed him and threw him on the floor in rough horse play, tickling and paddling him. Mollie forgot she had on only a gown and jumped up to try to stop it because she was worried about their ruining Jim's new suit. They thought this so funny that they had to stop for laughing and soon they left to go spread all over the neighborhood the story of the bride who had gotten out of bed in a gown to protect her husband's clothes. To keep her from feeling so bad over it, Jim bought her a new, crepe dress in town the next day on their way out to his parents' tenant farm, where they were to live.

Five years later Mollie was pregnant for the third time. She felt very hopeful because this was "the kickingest baby you ever felt." Her first child had been a girl, but a terrible disappointment to Mollie in looks. At four she was big, cumbersome, awkward, and slow moving, resembling her two-hundred-pound father so much that he was frequently told, "You couldn't deny that child if you wanted to!" The second baby was a boy, weakly and always crying just like the little brother Mollie used to sleep with and take care of. The alertness of the child she was now carrying promised better success.

Mollie showed more interest in everything that spring and summer. Jim's family had left them to go live and work in a cotton mill town and for the first time they were "tending" a farm and living in a house alone. Their family of four was the smallest she had ever cooked, cleaned, and washed for, and their tobacco crop looked good in July. She was glad Jim was raising tobacco instead of cotton because it meant more money in the fall. He was still kind about buying her one Sunday dress every year with the first tobacco money he got. Mollie was still pretty at twenty-three and during her nine months of pregnancy she often daydreamed of the child, who was to be a pert, attractive daughter whom she could dress daintily.

In midsummer when her time was nearing, the baby suddenly stopped moving one night, "right short like." Mollie knew that minute the baby was dead and alarmed she woke up Jim and told him about it. He reassured her, but on her insistence the next morning went to town and told the doctor about it. The doctor said there was nothing to do but wait, although it was eleven days before labor set in. The delivery was difficult for the dead fetus had begun disintegrating. The body was too much in pieces to be dressed for burial but they showed Mollie the face of her little girl and she thought it was the prettiest she had ever seen. Blood poison, complications, and a long illness afterwards made Mollie temporarily infertile and she had no more children for ten years.

At thirty-seven Mollie is again pregnant. She is not bitter about it, although she wishes doctors would tell you what to do when they say, "Now you shouldn't have any more children." She was quite surprised when she found she was "that way" four years ago, but she made up her mind she wouldn't hope or imagine anything because, "it's like counting your chickens before they're hatched." Then, too, Mollie has had many lessons in disappointment since her baby died. Several years there was not enough money even to "pay out," much less to buy the annual Sunday dress. Jim can't understand why he hasn't been able to buy a team. Of course, his labor force is small, but Mollie and the oldest daughter do almost full-time work in the summer. He has moved from one place to another in several counties trying to change his luck, but it has done no good. Mollie's greatest disappointment, next to the death of her pretty baby, was the year when they were living in a county where the land is supposed to be the best in the State for tobacco. Jim decided his luck had changed at last, for a week before time to begin priming, his tobacco was looking the finest of any crop he'd ever raised. He was so confident over the proceeds it would bring that he promised to give Mollie not only a finer dress than usual, but a permanent wave as soon as they sold the first load of tobacco. Mollie's straight hair had always been a source of dissatisfaction to her and she felt an almost girlish glow of anticipation over the thought of curls. Then hail came and tore the leaves, battered down the stalks, and ruined their tobacco crop. They had to sell their cow that year to pay up what they owed their landlord for furnishing.

And so Mollie, hoping no longer, was none the less delighted when her fourth child was again a pretty girl—not so pretty as the dead one, and a little plump, but much more nearly a replica of herself. Mollie began selling eggs to bring in a little money all during the year so she could buy cloth to make her daughter pretty clothes. At three now the little girl, always clean and dainty with a hair ribbon, seems incongruous with the meagerly furnished, not too well kept, three-room log cabin in which the family live. Mollie has already laid down the law that this child shall never have to do field work or heavy household tasks. She must go to school regularly and get an education so she can get a job early—"maybe a beauty parlor job"—and get away from farming with its hardships.

The other children are still trials to Mollie. Her other daughter is healthy and husky and "a mighty good hand," but she is eighteen now and has no beaus yet. She stopped school at fourteen in the fifth grade when they moved one year. She had always been "slow in the head" and failed to pass so often that she didn't want to go any more. She is good help to both her mother and father, but Mollie can't see why God gave her such a homely daughter. The boy is still in school and fairly "shrewd" at it, but he's nothing but trouble at home, always complaining about headaches and dizzy spells and getting out of work.

Mollie doesn't worry too much about the child yet to be born. She is sorry about the trouble it will be, but she accepts the "Lord's will" here as she does when they have a bad crop year. She no longer expects to realize the goals of life herself, but has transferred her efforts to achieving them for her daughter. Last year she even chose to forego the Sunday dress in order to buy a fur-trimmed coat for her baby. And yet Mollie is cheerful, except when impatient with her two older children, and works routinely at her farm and housework without complaint.

Chapter 14

Of Middle Age and Mother Worries

IN THE CASE of Mrs. Mary Hunt Simmons, a middle-aged tenant mother, quite tall and commanding in appearance, we have a symbol of another group of mothers. Her long, brown hair is combed straight back to a firm and respectable knot. Her features are strong and she is rather handsome except for bad teeth. She moves with vigor and talks with intense interest in what she is saying. She has an air of being alert and efficient, which her house, her canning display, and her neatly-dressed children confirm.

The stories of Mollie Goodwin and Mary Hunt illustrate the effects of the same pattern on two very different persons. By the "pattern" we mean those aspects of tenancy which are basic and almost universal—the low level of living with its associated deprivations, the lack of opportunity to achieve economic security, the necessity of continual hard work demanded by farms and large families, the tradition of patriarchal family organization with its associated sex mores.

In spite of contrasting personality traits, emotional development, and major goals in life, these two women—Mollie Goodwin and Mary Hunt—share by now certain similarities in outlook, forced upon them by the common elements in their situation. The major features in Mollie's girlhood were her love for pretty clothes and the rigid severity of her father; in Mary's, her striving by industry and thrift to compensate for the lack of her mother's affection, which was lavished on a younger, prettier sister. Marriage meant disillusionment for Mollie because it brought children and work rather than pretty clothes, and she accepts without zest her husband and the never-ending round of duties. Mary rejoices in her marriage and in her rather weak husband, whom she dominates within the forms prescribed by tradition, and focuses all her energies on making a living by industry and on maintaining respectability by guarding her children from the pitfalls of sex sins. Yet both are somewhat resigned to the fact that their economic goals cannot be achieved, both justify their acts by moralizations, both are mildly discontent without being bitter, and both reacted with pleasure to the opportunity of talking out past dreams and disappointments and present problems.

Mary relished the idea of telling about her life. The only condition she stipulated was that she could also tell of her "problems" with her children and ask for advice. On a fall afternoon she sat beside the stove in her sitting-bedroom and began the account.

Her mother and father, "mama and papa" to her, came from another county, where they were both brought up. They married there and farmed on shares for a good many years. They saved a little in the years that cotton brought good prices and bought a team just before they came to this community. They moved several times afterward, but never very far away and this locality has always been home to Mary.

Mary, the middle child in her family, was born here. Her mama had eleven, but the oldest and youngest were burnt up when they were babies, and the next to the youngest died soon after he was born, so that left just eight. In order, there were four pairs of children—the two oldest boys, then two more, then Mary and her sister Fannie, and then two younger brothers. The oldest child was burnt up in the other county just after he had learned to walk. His mama had gone out to milk and there was nobody in the house with him. He found a tow sack lying on the floor with a few Irish potatoes in it, emptied it and put it on over his head. This kept him from seeing where he was going and he walked right into the open fireplace. His mama came running when he screamed, but the sack had caught on fire and he had already swallowed some flame. He died that night, although his body wasn't very badly burnt.

Mary doesn't remember any of the children being born except the last two. The next to the last one was born in the afternoon and her aunt took all of the children off to the pasture. Just before suppertime her papa came for them and told them there was a new baby at the house. They rushed home to see it and were very proud of it, but it died that night. She remembers fewer details about the birth of the last baby, but she does remember how crazy they all were about him, especially since the baby just before him had died. The night before this last one died—it was May and the moon was up early—he looked out and said, "Whoo-hoo, look at the pretty moon!" And none of them could remember anyone ever telling him what the moon was; they figured he just knew it by himself. The next morning he and one of the other younger boys were not feeling very well and their mama left them lying on a pallet when she went out to help pick cotton. Nobody knew just how it happened because the other boy was asleep, but they guessed the baby was tossing and rolled into the fire. He must have run and jumped on the bed because it was burning too when the older boys got there; they were nearer the house than the baby's mama. She was very sad over this second tragedy and grieved for years over losing him because he was her last baby. Mary thinks the tragic loss had something to do with her mama's health because it was never very good after that. She didn't go to the field much afterward, because by then she had so many boys to take her place, but she always liked working outdoors.

For a long time Mary has realized that her mama and papa

were very different. He was more like George (Mary's husband); if he was going to do something he would just go on and do it—easy-like. But if her mama was going to do something, you would know about it two days ahead of time from her talking about it. She had a high temper, too, which Mary believes she inherited from her. Mary used to be very cross and sharp and would fuss about the smallest things when she first married until her husband cured her of it by being so gentle and rubbing her down and patting her back. Mary's mama did all the whipping; her papa never touched her. Mary remembers one time when they had to go up the road a piece to an uncle's for water because their well was no good. Her mama said, "Now when I send you for water, you go get it and come straight back; when I send you to play, I'll tell you." Mary went for water and stayed to play with her cousins, and so her mama came after her. She turned Mary right up and "burnt her up" with a shingle. Mary was terribly embarrassed because a little neighbor boy was standing right there looking at her getting spanked. Mary's mama spanked her frequently both in private and public, but Mary says she always loved her mama the most, nevertheless.

With so many brothers for associates, especially the two just older than Mary, she was brought up pretty much like a tomboy. Her papa raised cotton but he also did trapping for extra money. There was much more uncleared land then and he set traps for mink and fox. During the season, the two brothers just older than Mary got up early every morning and went down to the river to see if there was anything in the traps. Generally they let Mary go along with them because she liked to follow them around. When they were about ten and twelve they learned to chew tobacco on these trips to the river but they did not let their mama know about it. They used to slip some out of the big box their papa bought tobacco in. Mary watched them and caught on to their hiding place on a sill under the front porch. After they left, she got the tobacco and took it to her mama and the boys got severe whippings for it. The next morning Mary started off after them—they had to carry a lantern to see—and after they got some distance from the house they stopped and gave her a good talking to. They said if she ever told on them and took their tobacco to their mama again, they would never let her go along to the river with them. Then they said they were going by the "raw potato patch" on this morning, and that if she would promise never to be a tattle tale again, they would let her go and eat some raw potatoes, too. She gave her solemn promise and never told on them again to this day.

The two oldest boys got the most schooling; both of them finished the seventh grade. The two just older than Mary finished the fifth, but neither Mary nor any of the younger ones got that far. Mary never went to school regularly, but she learned to read and write and was in the Fourth Reader when she stopped.

Mary never fussed with her brothers although they would often tussle. A favorite pastime when they came home from the field for dinner was for them to try to get something away from her. They had lots of fun almost "wrastling." Mary did fuss with Fannie, her only sister, who was just two years younger than she. Fannie would not do things right because she was spoiled, and Mary used to slap her. When they were sweeping yards or making beds together, Fannie's sloppiness would make Mary angry because, Mary says, she has always been "sort of old-maidish." When she slapped Fannie, Fannie would call her mama and tell on Mary. Their mama would say, "Well, Fannie, if you can't please Mary, just come on in the house and let her finish sweeping all the yards by herself." And so Mary always did much more of the work than Fannie because her mother was never fair about it. Fannie had to do more when she got married, but even then she had some nearly grown stepdaughters who lived with her and did all the washing and heavy housework. And Fannie always kept her children out of school if there was anything that needed to be done at home.

Mary's parents finally achieved owner status when she was about ten years old. Her papa's grandfather's second wife, who was ninety-four years old, was living on a farm her husband had left her. She had no children and had been alone for quite a while. She used to visit around and stay a few days or weeks at one place and then at another and longest of all at Mary's family's house. Her nephews were her heirs and one spring they said that if Mary's parents would take her to live with them and if they would sign notes for a certain amount of money, they could have the farm. The house on it had six rooms while the one they were living in had only two with a sort of shed built on for the kitchen. Mary's mama had been saving and planning to go to Baltimore to visit for years, ever since some of her people had moved off up there. Her husband said to her, "Which would you rather do—spend the money to go to Baltimore and wait till we get some more in the fall, or spend what you have to roof the house so we can move in and live with Grandma now?" She decided she would rather give up the trip and move; her still increasing family was getting very crowded in the little tenant house they were living in. And so they moved in and the grandma died the next February. Mary's papa kept paying on the small farm almost all his life and her mama lives there now with one of her married sons, since her husband died.

Mary's papa wasn't what you'd call a hard father on his children. When they got old enough to go to parties and have them, he always let them have one lemonade-drinking every summer. These lemonade-drinkings were sometimes on Saturday nights, but most of the get-togethers of young people, with or without refreshments, were on Sunday afternoons. Almost every Sunday afternoon they met at someone's house. If the weather was good, they played out in the yard, hide and go seek, drop the handkerchief, and games like that. But after dark when they sat in the house, they could not play games because it was Sunday night. They sang often; the grandmother left Mary an organ and, when the gatherings were at her house, her papa loved to come in and hear the young folks sing hymns. Before they left, the boys and girls always planned whose house they were going to the next Sunday. Mary's brothers usually took her, or sometimes a neighbor boy who stayed with them and was so much like a brother to her that he never had hard feelings if somebody else wanted to come home with her.

Mary had known George all her life. He was just two years older than she and used to play with her brothers when they were all little. She supposes you'd say he started courting her when she was thirteen. That Christmas he sent her a little pin with a cross on it for a present and her brothers teased her so about it that she never wore it. She told them, "I don't care nothing about that little bowlegged George!" who was still wearing short pants at fifteen. From that time on he came visiting often. He never said he had come to see Mary but just sat around until bedtime with all of the family. He never talked much. Mary saw him at parties, too, and sometimes he would come home with her. When she was sixteen, they "busted up" because of another girl, who was crazy about George. This girl wrote Mary a card with, "Will you marry me?" on it and with George's name signed to it. Back in those days people didn't write insulting things on cards for everybody to see. Mary recognized that it wasn't George's handwriting, but she was so angry at him for letting the other girl do it and sign his name that she wouldn't have anything to do with him for nearly a year. Then one night at a party the neighbor boy who had "carried" her came and told her that George wanted to take her home. Mary said she didn't know whether she wanted to go with him or not, that they were angry at each other. And so George himself came and asked her so humbly that she gave in and went home with him. They were all right after that and got married in about a year. There were plenty of other boys paying Mary attention, but she didn't care anything about any of them except George.

George asked for her. He said it was the hardest thing he ever had to do in his life, but Mary declared that she wouldn't slip off to marry even if she had been fourteen. (The implication is that girls who marry before eighteen often slip off because their parents can prevent them from marrying if they know about it. After a girl is eighteen, or "free," there is no need for slipping off.) George didn't tell his own people, although his daddy must have known because he gave George some money. His mother was the sort who would be angry about something like that and yet be proud of it at the same time. Mary refused to go to his home for the first night and so they stayed with his cousins. The next day his daddy sent for them in a buggy and they went to live with his people for four months. After that they started housekeeping by themselves but kept on farming with George's family, who were share tenants. Wherever his daddy moved, they moved too, and lived in a little house if there was one; if there wasn't, Mary said "they sometimes lived in the back house." They kept farming with George's parents until his daddy died and his mother moved into town to live with a married son. This son makes about $30 a week and Mary thinks they ought to live well, but his wife is such a spender and buys everything on time, which means paying about five prices instead of one. Mary was there this summer and saw two pairs of curtains the wife had paid $10 for, when you could have got them for cash for $2 or $3.

Mary's mother-in-law quickly got over being angry about the marriage and was very good to Mary. She taught her to sew during the four months they lived together. Mary's own mother had never let her use the sewing machine just as Mary now doesn't let her daughters use her own. Mary guesses this is wrong because girls should have training, but she is so proud of the way she has kept her machine. It was bought twenty-two years ago second hand for $25 and in all that time she has never spent a cent on it except for one new belt and four packages of needles. She has done all their sewing on it because she learned rapidly how to do all sorts of sewing from her mother-in-law. She had four quilts made before she married and a few pillowcases and embroidered things. Once her papa gave her forty cents when she went to the fair, but she simply couldn't spend it on wasteful pleasures. Instead, she took it to town the next time she went and bought with it unbleached cloth and some wide lace, which she made into the prettiest pair of pillowcases to save till she was married.

Mary's first baby came before she had been married a year. Four more came with two years between as regularly as the years rolled around. Still another four, farther and farther apart, have been born, the baby, which Mary hopes will be the last one, when she was forty-one. All are living and all except Bess, the oldest, are at home. Mary never had much trouble when she was pregnant. For about six weeks each time she was pretty nervous, but then got to feeling better than usual, and always kept right on working to the last. She picked cotton straight through the fall until after Thanksgiving when her first child was born in January. She always had a hard time having babies, however; only once did it take her less than two days. A good old-fashioned country doctor brought them all; Mary thinks he knows what to do to ease you better than these hospital doctors do. And yet he never gave her any of that seven-minute medicine as he did to Fannie. When she got so worn out she begged for it, he always said no, she could have babies without it because she was stronger than Fannie.

Mary had the hardest time of all with her seventh baby. She lost her water one afternoon, but didn't get sick immediately. When Bess came home from school, Mary told her to start getting hers and the younger children's things packed up because they might have to leave before morning—she always sent her children off when she had a baby. After the menfolks had gone to sleep that night, Mary and Bess stayed up and finished packing and getting everything ready. About one o'clock Mary's pains started and she woke up George and told him to go take the children to their aunt's and get the doctor.

George brought back Mary's sister-in-law, who always stayed with her, and the doctor came soon afterwards. He examined Mary and said the baby wouldn't be born before the next afternoon. Mary told him to go on home, that she didn't want to give him breakfast unless she had to, and tried to make a brave show. She was terribly worried, however, because she had never lost her water so far ahead of time like that. The next morning the sister-in-law cooked breakfast and George went off to work. The doctor came back and told her to stay up as long as she could and to walk around and exercise. So she walked all the way down to the strawberry patch, although she was having hard pains every three or four minutes. As she came back across the yard, a pain hit her and she fell and struck a chicken coop, which bruised her badly. Her sister-in-law insisted that she stay in bed after that. As soon as she put on her gown and got settled in bed, some ladies came in to visit.

They knew she was expecting but did not know her time had come. While they were sitting there talking and laughing, the doctor drove up again. One asked, "Are you sick?" and all of them nearly flew out of the room when she said yes. As much as she was suffering, Mary had to laugh at them for being so embarrassed over being there when the doctor came; she did feel smart over not having let them find out that she was already in labor.

The doctor stayed this time and George went for the colored woman they always hired to help when Mary had babies. It was still more than twenty-four hours before the baby was delivered, and Mary says she has never suffered so in all her life. She begged the doctor to give her something; she was so sore and aching from the fall that she thought she couldn't strain against the pains any longer. He firmly refused, though, and she finally bore the baby the next night.

With her first baby, Mary didn't have enough milk and didn't know about bottles so she fed her right from the start—just chewed up for her whatever the adults were eating. Mary knows now this must have been very hard on the baby and she thinks it is one of the reasons why Bess has never been so healthy or so big for her age as the others. Bess had to stop high school four months before she finished because she had been menstruating steadily for nearly three years. Mary worried about it so that she nearly went crazy and it seemed that nothing would stop it. Finally the doctor started treating her with hypodermics and after several months of taking shots she stopped flowing and got well entirely before she married about two years ago. She has fine twins now herself and hasn't had any more female trouble.

The other children have been pretty healthy. George was especially helpful about watching out for them. He is the one who always remembers to make them put on their caps and coats so that they won't catch cold. Mary thinks sometimes that he is too careful. He used to have the idea that they shouldn't sleep on the feather bed because then if they spent the night away from home, they would catch cold from the change. Mary thought this was going too far, and so she let them change around so that they wouldn't get too accustomed to any one bed and now they can sleep anywhere. Last year all the little boys were wearing short pants to Sunday School, and every time the seven-year-old boy changed to them from the overalls he wears every day, he caught a cold. And so his father bought some knickers and long socks for him and, if he ever sees his son on Sunday with just the tiniest piece of his leg showing, he reminds him to pull up his stockings. Of course, Mary realizes that it's all in what they're used to because her girls wear anklets all winter long.

While George is much more careful of their health, it is Mary who has to do all the whipping. George just says, "Well, you're good and do your best, and I do, so the children are bound to be all right," and doesn't feel there is much need to do anything about it. And they do mind him even though he won't do any punishing. The children have never done much fussing among themselves, either. Mary says that a person like herself would fuss, but not George, and so they haven't seen much from their parents.

They both believe in giving their children all the education they can, although neither of them nor any of their people had very much. Mary is sorry to say that her brothers and sisters don't feel the same way about it she does. Fannie never felt it was important to get her children in school before Christmas. She would say to Mary, "You sacrificed yourself and never even kept Bess out to help with washing or anything. Now she's married and how much better off is she for having gone to school?" But Mary says you can't tell when a girl will have to make a living and those with education get the jobs. Then you can tell a person's education from his talk—she knows she talks "flat," she never had much. But her brother's sons talk just like a "nigger"; two of them can't even read and write. She was never more embarrassed than once when they were about thirteen and fifteen and were at her house waiting for Sunday dinner. She suggested that they read the funny paper while they waited and the oldest one said, "You know I can't read, Aunt Mary." Mary certainly went after them about it. She got clothes given to the children if the parents would let them go to school. Sometimes she lost her patience and threatened to put the "welfare" on them. She did get some of the children in school; one girl and one boy of her brother's are finishing high school this year just because she talked to them and gave them clothes and got them set on going. Last year she persuaded the principal to get some work for the boy and he filled the tanks of the school buses an hour a day and got $8 a month for it. This year after his father died, he came to Mary and said he just couldn't go on, so she went to the principal again and arranged for the boy to have a job in town on Friday afternoon and Saturday. He makes enough so that he can go to school during the week. Mary is certainly proud of those two children finishing because they never got one word of encouragement from their parents. In fact their mother has been furious with Mary at times for insisting that they go, but she would always get over it quickly.

Mary says she has always had a long tongue—they started her to begging for money for missions when she was in the Second Reader. She could never talk in public—her heart just fails her in meetings—but she can and does present other people's troubles to folks in town she knows—butter customers and others—and gets them to help out with clothes and books and things. And yet in Mary's opinion, it's not the lack of clothes that keeps most people from sending their children to school. They just can't see the importance of it and they seem to think there shouldn't be any question about their staying at home until the cotton is picked, the corn shucked, the sweet potatoes dug, and everything else done the children can help with. Mary sadly called attention to the fact that these are her own people she is talking about—they just can't see the value of an education.

There was never any question about her own children going. Mary and George never kept them out a day in their lives no matter how much the cotton needed to be picked. Of course they have their children work steadily in the field all summer, and on Saturdays and in the afternoons after they come home from school in the fall. Mary has also tried to train her daughters to do every single thing about the house except sewing, although they never help her a great deal because she won't keep them from the field if they're needed there. They have done pretty well at school, too; the oldest nearly graduated, and the next one did graduate last year. Five are in school now and the two youngest haven't started.

Mrs. Simmons asked if she could talk about her children now. She wants so much to raise them to be respectable citizens and a mother does worry so over every thing that happens to her children. She has always told them they have nothing to be ashamed of just because they have come from a poor family; if only they act right, they can hold their heads as high as anybody. One by one, she discussed her children, their weaknesses and good points, their failures and achievements.

For instance, Louise does well in her books except one year when she got behind in arithmetic. It has always been hard for her but, after the principal gave her some special help, she caught up. He lets her do office work for him in return, greet visitors, make lists, and things like that. She cannot be paid NYA money for it because she is too young, but the principal says it is good experience for her. In connection with Louise, Mary worries most about a little village girl who has been so friendly with her. This little girl carries on with boys shamefully at school parties and Mary wishes Louise would see through her and stop going with her. Mary won't allow her daughter to spend the night with her but they see each other at school every day. Louise is very good at home about helping Mary around the house and everybody says Mary should be proud of her. They had a contest at school not long ago and Louise got seven of the best things: best ability to meet people, most popular, most attractive, and some others. Mary has tried not to let Louise know how proud she is about it because she's afraid it might give her the "swell head."

Of all her children, Mary is now most worried about Georgie, her second oldest child. He thinks he wants to be a bus driver and his uncle can probably get him appointed to take the training course. Georgie says he has seen his parents nearly killed on farm work without getting anywhere and he doesn't want to be killed himself. Mary doesn't mind his doing some other sort of work, but she is worried about his hanging around the bus station; she has heard they do a lot of drinking when they come off the run. And that is one thing they have never had in their families—neither George's nor hers. When Georgie goes out at night and comes back in, Mary waits until he's asleep and then goes in and smells his breath to see if he has been drinking, but so far she's never detected anything. She doesn't want him to leave home yet, although he says he will come home to sleep if he can get the job. But Mary knows he could come home at two or three and tell her he had just come in from his run and she would have no way of knowing whether it was the truth or not.

She worries so about his getting in trouble with girls, too. She has tried to bring him up right; she has tried to teach him to be a Christian and has told him he *can* control every part of his body. He is going steady now with a nice girl, but she is just seventeen and her mother lets her go out at night with him. Mary wishes the mother were as strict as she is with her daughters—Bess never left the yard with a boy after dark till she was married and none of the younger ones will, either. Neighbors tell Mary the girl's mother thinks a lot of Georgie but Mary wishes she wouldn't trust him so much because they're both so young and girls will be girls and boys will be boys. She tells Georgie over and over that he must remember that he has been brought up right and not get in trouble—if he does, he can't bring it home with him on account of Louise and the younger ones, because they are going to be brought up right. Mary wishes her husband would advise him and warn him, but when she tells him to, George just says, "Oh, he'll come out all right—don't go worrying about him."

Young folks learn so much now from cheap books. Mary found the worst pamphlet in Georgie's pocket. It was the dirtiest thing; she had never known they printed such awful things. She showed it to George—she never keeps anything from him—and told him he should burn it up or tell Georgie to, but he's never done anything about it. Mary is ashamed to speak to Georgie about it herself, because of what's in it and because he would say, "What were you doing in my pockets?" Mary did show it to her married daughter and asked her where she supposed Georgie got it. The pamphlet had all sorts of things in it about using rubbers and pictures of birth control things, some sort of silver ones. Bess said she bet he got it at the filling station where he hangs out on Saturday afternoon.

They sell such things there and the drummers come around with the supplies and give away these dirty pamphlets. Mary just hopes that is where he got it and not somewhere else.

She wants him to stay at home one more year anyway. There is enough on the farm to be done to keep him busy even during the winter, but she is afraid he is going to get restless even though he's counting on doing a lot of hunting. He was talking to her yesterday and said he could be of more help to her and George if he had a job than if he just hung around here now that the crop is finished. She protested that if he had a job, he would probably spend his money just like Bess' husband, but he said he would expect to pay her some of it since he would keep on sleeping here. And Mary thinks it is right that he should help if he starts making anything.

Mary wouldn't worry about Bess for herself, it's all on account of her husband and the way he spends money. Of course she did a great deal of worrying about her daughter eleven months ago when her babies were born. It was the worst case Mary has ever seen; poor Bess was in labor for a week. Two women around here had died in childbirth this year and that made all the family even more worried about Bess. They thought she was dead once, and the twins, too, but they all pulled through and the babies are fine and healthy now. Corey, Bess' husband, is a smart boy and as good a worker as you ever saw. Last year he made $1200 off his tobacco—only half of it was his, of course—and this year $1400. He hasn't had to hire much help because Bess did most of the grading, although she couldn't work in the field much this year with her two young babies. His fertilizer bill and debt were less than $200 this year, so he cleared $500. Mary thinks he should have saved at least $300 of that—but it's all gone now, and not even Christmas yet. Mary knows there will be times when they will need to have something put away—trouble always comes—and they won't have it. And yet she hates to say anything, even to Bess, because she doesn't want to cause any trouble between them.

Bess is as thrifty as can be, but she doesn't have a chance to save. It's not that Corey isn't good to her; he bought her a sewing machine, a kitchen cabinet, a china closet, and some china this year. Bess was proud to get all these things, but she told Mary she'd a sight rather have put some of the money away. When Corey sold his tobacco, he gave Bess $50 for her own. She was very careful and didn't spend as much as she really needed so she could save some of it. Then after he had spent his own money, Corey began to borrow a little here and a little there until now hers is all gone, too. Bess says that next time she might just as well spend all she can get and let him buy her anything he wants to, because if he has anything left, he'll throw it away. As soon as he got his first tobacco money this year, he bought a car. Now Mary doesn't mean that it wasn't good business, because he has a trailer and has hauled lots of tobacco to market and gets $8 a trip. Then he's always thinking up things to do—he got a saw which runs attached to the motor of the car, bought up some "outsides," cut them, sold them for firewood, and made nearly $100 from it in two weeks. He is always on the lookout for extra things to do to make money, but then as soon as he gets it, it burns his hands till it's spent.

Mary guesses it was his raising. He was brought up poor just like her own children and never had much to spend, but his parents just didn't teach their children to save what they had. Whenever Mary begins saying anything to him now about his spending, he just shuts up as quiet and won't answer a word. When she tries to talk to Bess, the only answer she gets is, "I'm not worried, Mama, and don't you go worrying about it. Corey is as good to me as he can be, and it seems like he can make money to spend." From experience, Mary knows what happens to everybody, and how bad the couple will be needing to have something laid away, some day. From the very first, she and George always saved a part of whatever they made. Of course, it always got used up, but then it helped them through their trouble.

Mrs. Simmons talked for several afternoons about her children. Her many worries over them focus around her two basic goals of life, economic security and respectability. The latter, at least, she sees as something to be achieved and maintained by conforming to the traditional mores, especially those relating to sex. Finally, she apologized for having strayed so long from her original narrative of herself and her husband. It was clear that she had delayed an account of their economic history because she does not like to face their failure in this sphere or its implications as to George's ability.

When Mary's "in-laws" moved to town, they left George the team. George and Mary continued as share tenants on the same place for a number of years and saved a little and began to dream of buying a farm some day. And then with the depression, luck turned against them—a mule died, the boll weevil was extremely bad for several years, Mary had pneumonia, and finally their savings were used up, the other mule "went under the hammer," and they were left with only a cow and their household furnishings. They moved to their present location as sharecroppers and their financial condition has been slowly improving since then. They have paid all their bills except the doctor's and they hope to be able to purchase a team next year. Mary is able to tell the facts of their hardship but is defensive about their being interpreted as George's fault.

Of course, Mary helps all she can. She has had one butter

customer in town for twenty-two years and takes or sends in four pounds every week. Whenever she has anything extra she takes that to town, too, and sells it from house to house. But all her patches failed this year—watermelons, cantaloupes, and tomatoes—and what she canned extra and a few flowers are about all she has to sell. Every year along in the summer if she saw the crop wasn't going to be much good, she would get busy and put up something to sell or stir around to help out in some way. Now Fannie just sat back and let her husband worry about where the groceries were coming from and never did anything to help out. She never knew how much her husband got from a crop or any of his business.

On the other hand, George and Mary plan everything together and tell each other whatever they spend for anything. If he gets some money and comes by the store and buys something, he'll say, "I spent such and such for tobacco and potatoes, and here is $5 to put away, and I'll keep the other $2 in my pocket." And when Mary goes to town she, too, tells him everything she spends. George keeps the money, of course—"I don't tote the pocketbook and I don't believe in a woman doing it." If Mary is going to town without him, she asks him for money beforehand and he gives it to her, but she never keeps any money unless he has asked her to put some up to save. They always plan together, though. Last week they were talking about going to the fair. Mary figured they would spend at least a dollar each and said she would rather save hers to put on a dress or suit to wear to P-T-A meetings. She doesn't do any society, but she does need something to wear to meetings besides cotton house dresses, which are the only kind she has now. George isn't quite so saving; he said they'd just as well go on and spend it because when they die, what difference will it make anyway?

Mary can't help thinking about dying because she's had so

much trouble in her family this year. First her brother just older than herself died, and then Fannie with her twelfth child, and her mama is getting pretty old and feeble. Mary walks over to see her every week unless she is terribly busy or there's sickness or something. Her mother always reproaches Mary, as old people do. When Mary first comes, she says, "I thought you had forgotten me. I've been feeling so bad that I was going to send for you today if you hadn't come." After Mary gets her to talking for a little while, however, she is very bright and cheerful and doesn't complain at all. Once Mary didn't go to see her for two weeks when Bess' babies were born and the next time she went, her mama cried and said that Mary didn't love her any more. Mary tries to be patient with her mama, but this upset her and so she asked how often Fannie came. Mary knew Fannie went only about once a year although she lived no farther away than Mary. Her mama wouldn't answer this question and tried to change the subject. Mary let it go because she doesn't feel bitter any more about her mama's always having loved and petted Fannie the most. Mary knows that she has always done the most for her, and that gives her comfort to contemplate. Her mama gets along pretty well with her daughter-in-law, who lives with her, but her mind is getting weak and she can't keep it on any one thing very long at a time. She had always milked and she kept her own cow until last year when the boys made her stop; they said it wasn't right for her to go out in the cold of winter. And so she started feeding the pigs. She said she had to have *some* animals to take care of. She doesn't do much inside the house. She gets a hammer and nails and starts out to mend the pigpen and in a few minutes she will be 'way off doing something else —she can't keep at one thing very long.

Mary's own health is not so good as it used to be. She often still works a half day in the field, but she has to rest a while almost every day. Since she had pneumonia, she flows so much when she menstruates and never stops under ten or twelve days. George says she ought to hire somebody for fifty cents a week to help her wash the heaviest things, but she can't bring herself to do it. She just can't have somebody else doing her washing—not so long as she's up and going. George's health is worse now, too, but he is the sort who won't complain or tell anybody when he's feeling bad.

Mrs. Simmons talked more, bringing the various threads of her life up to the present. As she finished, she offered in summary, "Well, it seems like all I've told you is troubles, but I guess poor people have plenty of them. And yet I tell 'em on account of George's disposition, I bet we have the happiest home in the county. If I can just raise my children up to go straight and be as good as him. . . ."

Part III · Meanings

Chapter 15

On Finding the Answers

WE HAVE referred, of course, to the significance and enormity of the problem of farm tenancy, we have indicated how well he tenant farm mothers symbolize the economy, and we have llustrated some of the more important aspects of the pattern of Southern farm tenancy in the case of selected tenant farm nothers of the Piedmont South. Before comparing these nothers with a similar number from the lower South, we ought o be sure that our conclusions are based upon sound methods of inquiry and our meanings interpreted only in relation to he facts covered by this limited study. Although there is a reat deal of evidence to indicate that further inductive studies vould confirm these conclusions as being accurate and general, ur first task is to be sure that the story we have presented ere is authentic.

What then are the facts of selection and perspective? The rea and the sample are as representative as is required for ne methods of analysis used. These mothers are living in group of counties in the Piedmont section of North Carolina, n area of about 8,000 square miles containing nearly 700,000 eople, which has been marked off as a laboratory for special udy by cooperating research agencies. In youthfulness and eproductive vigor of the people this area is more "Southern" an the Southeast as a whole—that is, it has higher fertility tes, more of its population in the younger age groups, and a rger ratio of dependents to producers. In many indices such tenancy ratio and percentage of Negroes in the population e area is almost identical with the Southeast. In other characteristics such as urbanization, illiteracy, per capita income and level of living, it is between the Nation and the Region In percentage of industrial workers it is higher than either th Southeast or the whole United States. Since such a large pro portion of the mill villagers have come from tenant farms, th subregional laboratory offers a compact area for study, wher the factors of industry and urbanization are forcing a new bal ance with agriculture and rural life. This Subregion seems t typify "the New South," where population pressure is grea but where there is already sufficient advance over "the Ol South" economy that the people are not so destitute as in cer tain deteriorating areas of the South.

One-third of all the workers in this Subregion earn thei living by farming, but, since their families are larger, 41 per cent of all the people live on farms. Slightly over one-half o the farm operators are tenants, three-fifths of these tenants ar white, and it is from this group of 16,389 white tenant farn families that the mothers were selected.

The problem of selecting the sample of tenant women to b visited was difficult. There is no listing of all white farm ten ants in a county or township which makes it possible to numbe the women and to draw a random sample of them by the con ventional techniques. Furthermore, it was impracticable be cause of the size of the area to traverse every road, stop a every fifth or fiftieth house, and ask if a white tenant mothe lived there. For reasons explained earlier it was preferabl not to visit women living close together and this made it inad visable to block off parts of townships as sampling units an choose certain units by random procedure. Also it was foun from exploratory interviews that rapport was more easily estab lished if the visitor knew the woman's name in advance an that much time was saved if only those previously identifie as to color, tenure, and status of motherhood were visited.

Therefore, it was decided to use referrals from cooperating agencies and individuals. These included county farm agents, home demonstration agents, farm security supervisors, public welfare officials, public school principals and agriculture teachers, landlords, merchants, doctors, a minister, and other tenant farm mothers. From the referrals offered, selection was made in such a way as to secure approximate representativeness of the whole area in three aspects: location, type of farming, and socio-economic level. The distribution by counties of the group selected is approximately the same as that for all white tenants of the area; the proportion of types of farming is approximately the same; and the ratio of sharecroppers to other tenants is about equal to that for all white tenants. The chief characteristic in which the group visited differs from the larger, unvisited group in the area is the fact that there are more children. Not only were referrals to childless women rejected (except in one case), but, since the referring agents knew the study related to mothers, they often thought first of those in their acquaintance with large families. A bias in this direction seemed appropriate since the study has as its major purpose the amplification of the meaning of high fertility levels.

But it is not enough to point out the typicality or the authenticity of the area or of the cases. The reader has a right to know whether the methods of inquiry were sound, how the conclusions were reached, and not only that the cases are real and living but that the results are scientific and dependable. For this reason we must describe frankly and accurately the general approach, the technique of gathering the data, and the exact processes of analysis and interpretation.

Although the field of demography or population is the primary emphasis and interest, data other than the conventional population measures of fertility, age distribution, and so on, are examined. The chief purpose of the study is not to add to the quantitative indices which can be extracted from the Census, but to give substance and meaning to the numerical descriptions. It is already well established that rural women in the South have a high level of fertility and a low level of living, but little is known of what these quantitative measures mean in the lives of the mothers and their children. Therefore, the effort was made to be both more realistic and comprehensive in a sort of attempt to get away from restricted statistical treatment and stereotyped "case studies," and yet to combine as far as possible some features of the statistical, case, and survey methods.

Preliminary work included first a statistical analysis of the regional and subregional variations in fertility, which served to locate and define certain groups of high fertility levels, and to examine the implications of fertility differentials with particular reference to the Southeast. (Mothers of the South: A Population Study of Native White Women of Childbearing Age in the Southeast, unpublished doctoral dissertation by the author, University of North Carolina, 1937.) Secondly, a compilation was made of data on the group of Piedmont counties available from Censuses and from reports published by various state departments. For the subregional laboratory, the Southeast, and the United States, comparative indices were computed relating to population, agriculture, industry, wealth, health, welfare, and education. These two preliminary phases of the study furnish the necessary background information on the subject of differential fertility and on the socio-economic characteristics of the specific area in which the study was made.

The actual first-hand gathering of data consisted of repeated visits made by the writer to the tenant farm mothers during a sixteen months' period of field work. The approach to the women on first visits was varied and modified to suit the occasion and the person, but the basic procedure was as follows: the visitor, knowing in advance the name of the woman, found her—as often in the kitchen, striphouse, yard or field as at the front door—introduced herself as Mrs. Hagood from Chapel Hill, stated that she was interested in women who live in the country and their problems of bringing up children, and asked if she might visit for a little while. The pattern of cordial hospitality described earlier usually brought an invitation to come in and have a seat before even this much explanation was given. Conversation began most frequently on some aspect of the immediate situation—children or work. During the visits certain questions were asked directly, such as "How many children do you have?" or "How is your health?" but, in general, questioning was avoided. Topics on which an expression of attitudes was desired were approached obliquely and the interview was kept as much as possible to a friendly, conversational, "just visiting" tone. No notes were taken during the first visits to the North Carolina group, but the visit was written up as quickly as possible after the interview and much of the conversation was recorded practically verbatim.

After a dozen or so such visits a brief face sheet was drawn up containing a mininum number of items—age, number and age of children, type of farming, tenure, etc.—which were secured from all women visited. After all of the Piedmont group had been visited and a preliminary analysis had been made of the data gathered, a three-page mimeographed schedule was constructed providing blanks for information on all the essential topics of the study. This schedule was used for the "Deep South" group of mothers and later for the Piedmont group when revisited. All of the Piedmont mothers were visited at least twice except for a few who moved away, and about twenty-five of them were visited more often—up to six times. The visits varied in length from a half hour to four hours with a modal length of about an hour and a half. There was an opportunity to talk privately with over half of the mothers; with the rest, children, husbands, relatives, or neighbors were never absent.

The field work in states other than North Carolina was done on a slightly different basis. In Georgia and Alabama, counties were chosen to include both Black Belt and non-Black Belt cotton areas, with one section where there is greater diversification; in Mississippi and Louisiana, both Delta and non-Delta areas were chosen. For reasons of time and efficiency only one referring agency was used in each county—in Georgia, Farm Security; in Alabama, Departments of Public Welfare; in Mississippi, Farm Security and Home Demonstration Agents; in Louisiana, Farm Security. In all these states only one visit was made to each mother and the interview was centered around the filling out of the schedule. And yet, even with this more mechanical technique, there was time for informal talk and the atmosphere of visiting was maintained as much as possible.

After these data were gathered, the processes of analyzing, interpreting, and presenting them varied for different parts of the study in order to extract the maximum meaning from the materials. For the settings in Part I, farms were selected which seemed to illustrate the various elements of the "pattern" of tenancy and certain of its modifications. Fuller agricultural and economic data were secured on these farms, often from the husband. These sketches of farms make use of the illustrative function of case studies.

For the body of the study, contained in Chapters 6 to 12 and dealing with the activities and attitudes of the tenant farm mothers, we have tried to adapt the case study method to amplify and to give substance and meaning to statistical descriptions. We have tried to utilize case material to afford a richer sort of description than quantitative measures can give and yet to avoid the superficial, stereotyped, sentimental, "case study" in which the interviewee often "puts over" on the investigator wonderful and colorful narratives. In order to analyze and present this material in a more scientific way than case material is usually treated, we have used the two statistical concepts best suited to material for which no measures have been devised—the mode and the range of variation. These two measures, one of central tendency and the other of dispersion, have the advantage of being easy to apply; without even ranking the various individuals with regard to a particular trait, one can often indicate what is the most common manifestation and what are the manifestations which vary most widely in either direction from this mode. Furthermore, these concepts have the advantage of indicating for qualitative material the features which have the most meaning in everyday thinking—the type, or most usual, and the limits of the group under investigation in a particular trait. Additional supplementation is made from other illustrative material at any point on the range, so long as it is approximately located regarding the mode and the two extremes as points of reference. Thus the mode and range operate as a balancing framework within which any material gathered may be presented.

This method of presentation avoids the featuring of pathological cases as typical, a frequent practice of novelists and playwrights who for artistic and dramatic effects distort reality in this way. And yet the method affords an opportunity for presenting pathological and other atypical material with an indication of its relative position. Furthermore, it continually stresses the important fact of variation within even a fairly homogeneous group and thus warns the reader to be cautious in applying stereotypes based on the "average" tenant farm mother to all members of the group.

In Chapters 13 and 14 we have used case material in "long

section" to illustrate the continuity of personality development in the tenant farm environment. Again this is the illustrative function of the case study, employed here with greater emphasis on subjective reactions than in Part I. Finally, in Chapter 16 there is a summary of the results of the quantitative comparison of the two groups of mothers for the purpose of showing to what extent the Piedmont mothers reflect conditions in the larger South.

From the use of these several methods, the conclusion seems justified that the results arrived at are fair and valid. In addition to those results which have been presented somewhat topically, chapter by chapter, we shall venture to make more general interpretations in the last chapter. There, along with a brief recapitulation of the findings, we shall point out the implications of the functioning of these tenant farm women for the whole Nation and the importance of this group in the matter of population "quality."

Chapter 16

On the Place of the Piedmont Tenant Mothers in the Larger Southern Group

In order that a broader perspective of the Piedmont tenant farm mothers might be secured, an approximately equal number of tenant women were visited in Georgia, Alabama, Mississippi, and Louisiana. This was done to ascertain how well the more intensive study is supported by findings in the "Deep South." In the following comparison of the two groups, fundamental similarities suggest certain invariants in the pattern of Southern farm tenancy and in the way of life of Southern farm tenant people, despite the recognized differences indicative of modifications caused by location, type of farming, and subregional folk differences within the larger Southern culture. On the whole, the basic problems are the same, even though they vary in the degree of intensity of their several aspects.

The summary of the comparative data presented here is not, it must be emphasized, a generalized, definitive contrast of all Piedmont tenant mothers with all other tenant mothers of the South. It should be emphasized there was a difference in the method of obtaining information from the two groups; the Deep South mothers were asked for the information presented in this chapter on the first and only visit to them, while the Piedmont group were not asked for such information until the second or later visits. It seems probable that more confidence can be placed in the data from the group with whom rapport had been better established. In spite of these limitations, however, the comparison seems to serve to suggest that many of the conclusions and interpretations of this particularized study are applicable to the broader regional problem. Moreover, it points out the existence of deviations in various phases of life of one subregional group from those of other subregions.

The two groups are of comparable size. There were in all 129 Piedmont women and 125 Deep South women, but since these included a few small owners, the actual numbers of tenant farm women for whom data are tabulated are 117 of the former and 124 of the latter. The different methods of getting referrals for the two groups have been explained. An effort was made to keep the economic levels of the two groups about the same, although the only direct measure of economic level obtained is proportion of relief cases which is about one-fifth in each area. The most noticeable effect of using different methods of getting referrals is in the higher percentage of farm security clients in the Deep South (15 and 65 percent) and in the modifications this makes in items affected by the farm security program. (Throughout this chapter, the first number or percentage in a set of parentheses refers to the Piedmont group and the second number or percentage to the Deep South group.)

Data on family history and on mobility show that the Piedmont group is more stable as to location. Nearly one-half of the tenant wives and husbands are living in the county of their birth and only a slightly smaller proportion in the county of birth of their parents, while only one-fifth of the Deep South group are residing in their native counties and an even smaller proportion in the native counties of their parents. The 45 Delta families visited were chiefly responsible for this, as only four of the wives and one of the husbands are natives of the counties in which they are now living. Approximately two-fifths of the Piedmont group are living in the same state in which they were born but in a different county, while about three-fifths of the Deep South group are in this category. Only half as great a proportion of the Piedmont husbands and wives as of the Deep South ones were born in states other than the one of present residence (10 and 20 percent). None of the husbands, wives, or their parents of the Piedmont group was born in a foreign country, while one wife and six parents of the Deep South group were not born in the United States. The mean number of years lived in the present house (4.5 and 2.4 years), neighborhood (14.0 and 7.6 years), and county (24.1 and 14.2 years), are about twice as great for the Piedmont as for the Deep South group. Along with measures of mobility in location, the measures of mobility in occupation are smaller for the Piedmont group. More of the husbands and wives have come from farming families (94 and 90 percent) and more of the farming families were tenants (78 and 57 percent). These indications of stability of the Piedmont group were substantiated by the frequency of references to family connections in the community and county and by many evidences of identification with neighborhood and loyalty to place.

In personal characteristics the differences in mean age (38.1 and 39.2 years), mean age at marriage (18.6 and 19.3), and in mean number of years exposed to pregnancy (17.2 and 17.3) are inconsiderable. The greatest differences are in educational level as measured by the mean number of grades completed (4.6 and 6.6 grades) and in fertility level as measured by the mean number of children per woman (6.3 and 5.6 children). A larger percentage of the Piedmont women have never had any occupation other than farming and homemaking (74 and 57 percent). The proportion of women who have worked in mills or factories is the same for both groups—just over one-fifth. The greater percentage of women who have had other occupations in the Deep South group is due in part to the packing and processing plants for peaches and peppers, where women may get seasonal work in the Georgia area visited, and in part to the greater percentage of ex-teachers in the Deep South (one and eight percent). More of the Piedmont women reported themselves as being in good health (48 and 29 percent)—a phenomenon which seems to be related to the greater prevalence of malaria in many of the areas visited in the Deep South. The incidence of pellagra (5.1 and 4.0 percent) is about the same for the two groups.

The greatest number of children per woman in the Piedmont group is accompanied by less advance in some of the details of upbringing: a larger proportion of babies delivered by midwives, a smaller proportion nursed by schedules, a larger proportion reported as "spoiled," a larger proportion taken to the field (of course the summer sun is not so hot in North Carolina as in the states farther South), a smaller proportion of school age children in school, and a larger proportion of those in school kept out for work and other reasons. These data are suggestive of the better advantages provided for children in smaller families where the economic level is about the same. Several families in the Deep South have children of high school age not in school because neither local schools nor transportation to town schools is provided. In two cases children are out of school because their parents can not afford to pay the tuition required of those children who live outside of town. All of the children in the Piedmont Subregion, however, have school facilities available to them, and the only economic reason for their not being in school is the necessity of working or the lack of enough money to buy clothes or school supplies.

Indices of level of living computed from Census and Market Data Handbook figures show that the Piedmont Subregion is somewhat above the Southeast as a whole. This higher plane of living is evident to some extent in the housing of the Piedmont tenants. Compared with those of the Deep South tenants, the houses have more rooms, more stories, are of better material, and in better condition. Although a count was not made, it seemed that more of the houses had been originally built for owners. The houses of the Deep South group, however, have more conveniences: more have screens (58 and 61 percent), more electricity (seven and nine percent), running water (none and four percent), radios (22 and 29 percent), phonographs (15 and 26 percent), and more are painted (34 and 37 percent). These indices, however, hardly indicate fairly the contrast between the Piedmont houses and those of the Delta, where the houses are by far the worst of any visited. Their construction is shabby and all improvements are kept to a minimum, especially where there is fear of floods. The modal Delta tenant house visited is a two- or three-room, box, "shotgun" house—one room behind another without halls. The slightly higher rating on screens does not mean very much, for exceedingly few of the screens were at all adequate or effective in keeping out flies and mosquitoes. Furthermore, the Delta mud does not make attractive yards; the most common complaint about the effect of location on housekeeping was the tracking in of "buckshot" mud in the winter.

In diet, the advantage of not being pressed for land in the tobacco growing Piedmont is offset somewhat in the Deep South cotton areas by the larger proportion of farm security clients, who are encouraged by supervisors in home production of food. More of the Piedmont group have chickens (96 and 90 percent) and fall or winter gardens (72 and 53 percent), while more of the Deep South group have cows (85 and 94 percent) and do canning (74 and 84 percent). The farm security program includes special loans for the purchase of cows and of pressure cookers for cannings. The percentage of tenants having fruit trees on their farms (29 and 36 percent) generally depends on conditions beyond their control, while the percentage having watermelons (64 and 71 percent) and stored sweet potatoes (56 and 64 percent) generally depends on the suitability of the soil for them—at least this reason was almost universally offered by the tenants who did not have them.

The greater proportion of cash tenants (6 and 57 percent) and the smaller proportion of sharecroppers (34 and 12 percent) in the Deep South group is also due to farm security policy to some extent. In certain states farm security requires its clients to rent for cash before they can get loans. Many of those in the Deep South group who own work stock (58 and 85 percent) have bought the stock with government aid, which has enabled families, only recently sharecroppers, to rise to the status of cash renters. Perhaps the most important differences with reference to farming between the two groups is in type of cash crop. While some of the Piedmont farms are cotton farms 19 and 98 percent), none of the Deep South farms are tobacco farms (73 percent and none). About one-third of the tenants in each group are on farms having only one tenant, about one-fifth of the Piedmont and one-tenth of the Deep South tenants on farms having more than 20 tenants, and the remainders on farms of intermediate size.

However, this distribution of farms by number of tenants is misleading for the Deep South. In the Black Belt and Delta counties visited, where the largest holdings are, many of the large owners either have only Negroes on their plantations or do not permit their tenants to use farm security as a credit source and, hence, were underrepresented. And yet the attitudes of the tenants living on smaller holdings in these areas are markedly affected by the concentration of land and wealth around them. It is here that the bitterest indictments of landlords and the system are voiced. The overrepresentation of tenants of the poorer, smaller landlords is also partly responsible for the need of supplementary incomes in the case of a greater percentage of tenants in the Deep South (43 and 67 percent). The fact that seasonal work on the levees for men in certain areas and in processing plants for women in others provides an opportunity for obtaining supplementary income is also partly responsible. In the matter of credit, the farm security clients again show up in larger proportion in the Deep South. In the Deep South there is a greater percentage of tenants who get credit for running expenses than for fertilizer, due to the fact that on many of the Delta farms the land is so rich that it does not require fertilizer. In the Piedmont Subregion the reverse is true; credit is almost always necessary for the large fertilizer expenditure invariably required, while running expenses may be met by selling produce or by some other means of supplementing the farm income. In regard to participation of the mothers in farming, a greater percentage of the Piedmont women work in the field (77 and 62 percent) and a greater percentage of them prefer field work (88 and 80 percent). Poor health, hot sun, and heavy land are some of the reasons given by Deep South women for not doing field work.

A larger percentage of the husbands of the Deep South women have worked at something other than farming (44 and 62 percent), probably because of the plight of cotton growers in recent years. More have worked at sawmills and at "public work," the catch-all category which makes the exact placing of occupations difficult. In matters relating to woman's status within the family, the mothers of the Piedmont Subregion seem to have some advantage: in buying groceries (18 and 10 percent), in buying clothes (61 and 45 percent) and in disciplining the children (87 and 70 percent).

In the practice of contraception, the Piedmont mothers are

somewhat less sophisticated (12 and 28 percent), although more of those who do not practice contraception approve of it (88 to 76 percent). Several of the Deep South mothers told of induced abortions, whereas the practice was never mentioned by the Piedmont mothers except to be condemned. This, of course, does not mean they have never induced abortions. One Deep South mother, who disapproves of abortion now, gave an account of how she was once tempted and swallowed eight buckshot for this purpose. The "recipe" did not work and she thinks the Lord punished her by sending her the twins which were the ultimate result of the pregnancy. In neither group does an appreciable percentage of the mothers want more children (three and eight percent). The most common reason given for not wanting any more children by the Piedmont mothers was "I got plenty already," and by the Deep South mothers, "We can't afford to raise any more."

The mean distance from town of the Deep South group is less than that of the Piedmont group (nine and seven miles), a fact which may have been caused by the referring agents' having given more consideration to accessibility. There was reason for their doing this, for while the distributions of the two groups by type of road are not greatly different (paved highway, 18 and 16 percent; improved dirt road, 50 and 44 percent; unimproved road, 32 and 40 percent), the plantation roads and bayous in the Deep South were much harder to traverse than the corresponding unimproved roads in the Piedmont Subregion. Their present location is preferred to other locations by about three-fifths of each group. More of the Piedmont women give "home" as reason for community preference (34 and 14 percent), whether the preference is for the present location or another; more of the Deep South women give "convenience" (19 and 32 percent); and about the same percentage of each group give "people" (31 and 33 percent). In the

Deep South, "convenience" or "conveniences" is given most often by those who live or had lived on the unimproved and often impassable roads, "land" by those who contrasted the Delta with the hill country in soil fertility, and "people" or "home" by those who contrasted the same areas in favor of the hills.

In the Deep South group there are more families who attend church four or more times a month (three and seven percent) and all of them are of the Holiness denomination. Since the visits to the Deep South group were made during the summer revival season, religion was a topic of greater current interest with all of them than with the Piedmont group. Some of them made strong cases for the Holiness religion, while others denounced it. There were accounts of miraculous healing and of children as young as seven "speaking with unknown tongues." Pamphlets as well as patient explanation about their religion were given to the visitor. More of the Deep South women belonged to some organization other than the church (13 and 26 percent), and this, too, seemed to be affected by the farm security program. The percentage of women who do not visit at all, however, is greater in the Deep South (10 and 30 percent) and seems to be associated with short length of stay in the neighborhood. Cornshuckings are not in the folkways of the Deep South families, nor is any other form of cooperative activity that could be discovered. The higher incidence of automobiles in the Piedmont Subregion (50 and 35 percent) can generally be traced to some one good tobacco year within the past decade, whereas cotton farmers have not been so fortunate. Many of the cars reported are not in running order now, and many of those in running order have no licenses in spite of the very low license cost in some of the Southern States.

We may now summarize the facts brought out in this comparison to see what they indicate about the place of the Piedmont tenant mothers in the larger Southern group. Most important is the conclusion that throughout the South the basic factors of low income, high fertility, and lack of social services produce a primary pattern of farm tenant life. Greater variations in this pattern are exhibited between individual tenant families in one area than between the group averages of different areas. In terms of groups, however, the Piedmont families as compared with the Deep South families are more stable, more "settled," have a slightly higher farm income, which is less frequently supplemented by part-time work, and live in sturdier homes, which are furnished with fewer conveniences. The Piedmont women have less education but more children and show a greater chronological lag in their methods of training and educating them. Accordingly, conclusions and interpretations made on the basis of this group of Piedmont tenant farm mothers, when extended to the whole South, would have to be modified only in degree of emphasis. Such conclusions would tend to exaggerate slightly the fertility of the group, but would underemphasize their economic straits; they would overrate them somewhat in stability, but would underrate them in chronological advance.

Thus, it appears that the more general conclusions of the next chapter are entirely valid for the larger group of Southern farm tenant mothers since the conclusions do not depend on measurement of the precise levels of these aspects. It seems true also that this study has demonstrated the use of a subregional laboratory in making social studies. The area chosen seems especially appropriate where the focus of emphasis is oriented toward constructive planning rather than toward an examination of pathologies as such; for it provides a laboratory where the agricultural base is not yet in a submarginal state; where the regional demographic characteristic of reproductivity and its associated problems of training children and youth are exaggerated; and where the fairly recent industrialization gives promise of evolving a new rural-urban balance, although as yet it has done little in modifying traditional rural folkways.

Chapter 17

On Interpreting the Facts

ONE NEEDS only to sense the reality of those powerful and eloquent expressions of the people indicated in the full page portraiture, gleaned from text and context, to see the types of problems involving the facts and situations portrayed in this volume. Facts of agriculture, of time lags, of rural ways, of economic insufficiencies—all these and many others impinge upon the life and functioning of the tenant farm mother.

In conclusion, we can but examine them once again in a search for the meanings and implications of this group of mothers for the Southeast and for the whole United States. Much more than local or merely academic interest attaches to the question, "What sort of women are these tenant farm mothers, symbol and reality of a working folk called upon to reproduce more than their share of the next generation?" Therefore it is especially important that our facts be interpreted in true perspective to as many related factors as possible; and that we do not claim for them more than is their due.

Throughout the study we have seen that the situation of the tenant farm mother is defined in terms of almost every imaginable adverse external condition. From truncated childhoods, with meager preparation, they begin prematurely the triple rôle of mother, housekeeper, and field laborer. They work in this triple rôle with all odds against them—past training, present technology, and future possibilities of achievement which might serve as motivation. And yet they function—producing and caring for families and crops—and by their very efficiency they mollify the pathological effects of the externally operating factors on their children.

In such a situation, survival and the achievement here portrayed can be interpreted as evidence of the existence of inherent quality, vitality, and endurance in the people, and of certain facilitating factors and enhancing values of rural life. The evidence is inferential, it is true, but at the present stage of science, there have been developed no adequate techniques for directly measuring either "quality" of people or "values" of rural life. Intelligence tests for the former and conventional economic indices for the latter are unsatisfactory partly because both have been invented and standardized chiefly with regard to Northern, urban, supertechnological civilization. Final and conclusive evidence must await the construction and application of adequate objective scales to these suggested elements of worth in a folk society. Until then, however, the weight of the present examination of a group of Southern people is toward strengthening the case for the appraisal of the human resources and the rural life of the South as assets.

However, there is no basis for laissez-faire optimism. We have shown that this segment of the South's human resources, which will be represented in succeeding generations by a much larger segment, has inadequate diet, housing, medical treatment, education, social life, and recreation. The solution to the problem of how tenant farmers may achieve incomes large enough to eliminate these disadvantages is a major task for the regional economist; our findings can only emphasize the urgency of attacking it. More particularly in regard to the special interest and emphasis of this study, we have shown that the burden of involuntary and overfrequent childbearing is great for these mothers and often endangers the health and welfare of the children borne. Here there are more promising beginnings of alleviation in the state-wide program of contraception inaugurated two and a half years ago by the North Carolina State and County Departments of Health and since then in the beginning of a similar program by another Southern State. But until the agricultural system of the South is successfully rehabilitated, or until family limitation practices become far more universal than at present, Southern farm tenant mothers will continue to supply a disproportionate share of children who will be disadvantaged from birth. And even though the finest inherent vitality be granted and the intangible values of rural life admitted, the environmental handicaps, both biological and social, are sufficient to prevent these youth from attaining the "quality" of population desired for American people.

We have seen that the general tenor of these conclusions holds for the larger group of Southern farm tenant mothers as well as for the Piedmont group. The essential features of the portrayal of the Piedmont tenant mother, multiplied many times, may serve as a first approximation to a description of nearly a million and a half tremendously important reproducers of the Nation's people. We do not deny or minimize the variations associated with racial or locational groupings, or even the variations occurring within such groupings. But regardless of such divergences, the basic fact still stands for the entire South: that its tenant farm mothers are performing the task of reproducing more than their replacement quota under economic and social conditions disadvantageous to themselves, handicapping to their children, and ultimately detrimental to the Nation.

The account which we have presented of these disadvantaging conditions and their effects shows that the basic fact of high reproductivity under such conditions is socially undesirable for strictly sociological reasons. This is by no means identical with the point of view of the alarmist eugenicists who deplore the propagation of the race by low economic groups such as tenants because of the transmission of innate, biological inferiority. On the contrary, we repeat that the evidence of this study points to the vitality and quality of these people, since an examination of their continued disadvantaging situation leads to such an evaluation on the basis of their having achieved even their present low level.

With the rate of reproduction decreasing rapidly in almost all groups of the Nation, these mothers of the South may become more highly esteemed for postponing the stage of a declining national population. But whether they be evaluated positively or negatively for performing this function, the fact remains that these mothers continue to produce and rear children under adverse but remediable conditions and that the policy of the Region and Nation toward the removal of such conditions will be a significant factor in the determination of the future generations of American people.

The import of the direction of policy regarding this stupendous problem may be deduced as follows. On the one hand, if we begin with the assumption of Secretary of Agriculture Henry Wallace that children from "poor-white shacks" transplanted by adoption can be made "as intelligent as you and I," and if we posit an effecting of such an optimum transformation of conditions, the difference between the resulting quality of people which would be wrought in the next and succeeding generations and the results which seem inevitable if present conditions continue would be tremendous. It might well be great enough to swing the balance in favor of survival of democracy. For, as Secretary Wallace points out, this opportunity of developing intelligence, or "quality," is truly, "the genetic basis of democracy."

On the other hand, if we should take the position at the other extreme from Wallace, that adopted by some academicians—namely, the assumption of a large degree of pathology with questionings about the intelligence and vitality of the people—the responsibility might appear to be even greater. For surely no intelligent statesmanship would either permit such an extraordinary opportunity for reconstruction of a sturdy people to lapse, or burden the future of the Nation with such handicaps of biological and cultural deficiency.

Thus it follows that the welfare and functioning of Southern farm tenant mothers have consequences of significance not only for the quality of people who shall inherit the Nation, but through them, eventually for the sort of Nation which will be maintained. In the end, the fate of a Nation together with its culture and its civilization rests upon its people. This outlook renders more reasonable and less far-fetched the enthusiast's, "As goes the rural mother of the South, so goes the Nation." And finally, it points to an immediate optimum focus for the ameliorative efforts of those who would insure for generations in advance the outcome of the Nation.

Index